Four More Tears

by
Daniella Lerner

FOUR MORE TEARS

© 2008 Daniella Lerner. All rights reserved.

First published by Ecademy 07/28/2008

Ecademy Press
6 Woodland Rise, Penryn,
Cornwall UK TR10 8QD
info@ecademy-press.com
www.ecademy-press.com

ISBN: 978-1-905823-42-0 (sc)

Printed and Bound by;
Lightning Source in the UK and USA

This book is printed on acid-free paper from managed forests. This book is printed on demand, so no copies will remaindered or pulped.

ACKNOWLEDGEMENTS

Writing this book has taken me on a journey that I could never have envisaged when I wrote that first word all those years ago. In the process I have leaned on and needed the support of so many.

I would like to thank my husband Martin for being there and supporting me in this project every step of the way, and remaining loyal to me even after reading things about himself that could not have been easy.

Many heartfelt thanks must go to my parents who when reading this account learnt of things that they were not aware of, and for the wonderful love and support they have given me throughout my life.

Stephanie, thank you is not enough to express my gratitude for being the sister and friend that you have been, for loving me totally and unconditionally, and for being a wonderful true friend.

Joanne, I credit you for being such an intrinsic part of my life. Thank you for all the support and love and for helping me through some of my darkest days without even knowing it. I love you always and no amount of sea could change that love.

My wonderful children thank you. Without you my life would be empty and lonely. You have all given me the strength and motivation to pursue this book and its consequences and I adore you all.

Nigel Risner, thank you for being my mentor and guide. Fate deals cards and brings people together for a reason. Without you I don't think this book would have happened. I will be eternally grateful.

To all my friends who have had to endure my obsessive compulsion during my writing months, and to all of you I thank you profusely for your encouragement and belief in me.

Lastly, I would like to thank Dr Jake McKinnon whose memory I dedicate this book to.

INTRODUCTION

Jodi is now nineteen years old, and for the last fifteen years I have meant to write a book. As I sit in our rather beautiful home, pictures of my little girls line the walls, and their toys and papers and all their little knick-knacks are strewn around every room. When I see them sitting around the kitchen table, laughing, singing, shouting and bickering, my eyes often well with tears, and I can not believe how wonderfully lucky I am.

Then I look into the eyes of my oldest child, and often see the wistful yearning on my husband's face, and sometimes when all are asleep, and the autumn smells are in the air, I remember that time, and I feel the empty gaping hole deep in my stomach. The scars that can never be repaired, the pain and grief of then, and the worry and often helplessness of now, and I wonder what the next twenty years will bring.

This book is about a journey that few people have experienced. Many have experienced maybe one or two of the hurdles and on reaching them have probably thought, "Am I alone in this?" or perhaps, "How can I go on?" or, "Do I want to go on?" I wanted to write this both for those people, and also for myself, as a way to finally lie to rest those ghosts that often play havoc with my emotions.

Writing this book has taken me on a journey, one that has been both uplifting and soul searching. I didn't expect that writing would open up and yet heal so many wounds and emotions. It has taken me many years to finally finish my story. Even though this story ends with the last chapter, my life goes on and with it so does my determination to succeed and overcome the challenges that life sets for us.

CHAPTER 1

W/hen I was seven someone told me that if you wished on the first star in the sky then your wish would come true. I used to stand waiting by the window watching the dusk fill the sky, searching for the very first star so that I could wish for the one thing that I wanted more than anything in the world. I used to wish that my china doll would come alive and that when I woke, instead of a lifeless, vacant, voiceless doll lying at the bottom of my bed, I would find my very own baby. A baby that would be only mine to look after, feed, change, cuddle and play with.

Each night as I closed my eyes, my wish so fresh in my mind, the thought of what might be in the morning leapt inside my head causing excited stirrings and expectations as I drifted happily and dreamily into blissful oblivion. Every morning I would lean over the end of my bed knowing exactly what to expect, but hoping beyond hope that this time would be different, that today would be the day that my wish had been fulfilled.

I don't remember actually giving up my star wishes. Life has a way of moving without you even noticing. I remember all my days being so full of loveliness. My sister Stephanie and I were more than sisters, we were friends and allies. I was her protector and she was often my voice.

We spent many hours and days in our make believe world of play, often only stopping to sleep. Even when we ate our meals we were in character.

Our home was a three-bedroomed semi-detached house in Kenton, Middlesex. Both my parents worked. My dad was a cinema manager and my mum a teacher in the school that I attended. They were wonderful parents and on reflection our lives were delightfully ordinary.

I adored my father in a way that I could feel it in my chest when I thought about him. When he took us to school I remember being so proud that he was my dad. He was tall and strong and I thought that he was the most handsome man on the planet. When he left us to drive off to work, leaving us to our day at school, I yearned for him and felt empty and deserted. I don't think that emotion has ever quite left me. I always believed and still do (irrational though it may seem) that my dad could always make everything fine.

I was eight when my baby sister Joanne was born. My prayers had been answered. She arrived in the summer holidays and I can still remember the smell of the white plastic carrycot that she came home in. She was beautiful and very noisy but there was nothing that I wouldn't do for her.

Stephanie and I moved out of the little room into the newly decorated slightly bigger room that had lilac walls and louvered cupboard doors, and Joanne moved into the little room with all her baby paraphernalia.

Seasons passed by uneventfully until at eleven we moved to Bournemouth as my dad was promoted and we were relocated. I was delighted as I had just started a huge mixed secondary comprehensive school, which I absolutely despised. I had come from a tiny primary school with ten to a class and was suddenly expected to cope with this massive new environment. I was ugly, skinny and very dark skinned. I was shy and had a distinct lack of self-confidence and self-worth, so all in all I was a fantastic target for the bullies. I think the three months spent at that school were the unhappiest of my life so far.

So when we were told that we were moving out I thought I had been saved!

CHAPTER 2

Living in Bournemouth was a little like being on a permanent holiday. I was enrolled into an all girls' comprehensive school, which although vast, was heaven in comparison to the one I had just left. Stephanie was too young for secondary school for another year yet so she went to the local village school, and Joanne went to the nursery that had been set up by my mum almost as soon as we arrived in Bournemouth. It was situated in the local synagogue.

We lived in Talbot Woods, which was about three miles from the centre of town. The roads were tree-lined and wide and the houses were much bigger than those we were used to, and everywhere I looked there was green.

My social life was centred around the Hebrew classes that I attended three times a week, and I made my closest friendships there.

I taught myself to play the guitar and began piano lessons. Then Stephanie, my "best" friend Michelle and I started our own group and named it Triangle. We started writing our own songs and performing in all sorts of salubrious places: old age homes, nursing homes, blind homes and the occasional church fete.

Eventually, we did start receiving recognition, so much so that at one performance at the "Winter Gardens" (which happened to be a real theatre) we actually received a request and then the audience gave us a standing ovation. It was at that point that we believed we were truly famous!

Throughout this entire rise to fame I was also becoming increasingly interested in the opposite sex. Michelle started dating the rabbi's son whom

I was madly in love with, so I had to settle for his best friend. But this had quite severe repercussions when he French kissed me on the Heath and I thought I was going to be sick as a result, all the time during the ordeal counting the seconds in my head until it was over and then heaving and crying all the way home. All this for a few extra moments with his best friend the rabbi's son! I even took up short-distance running so that I could go and train with him, and as it turned out I was actually quite fast and ended up running for the school team.

Time passed quickly in Bournemouth and my interests in potential boyfriends altered frequently. However, I was not particularly attractive and not very happy in my own skin. I always felt that everyone else was better than me in looks, talent, academics and anything else that sprang to mind. So my lack of self-esteem didn't really help towards making me very good girlfriend material.

School days were spent writing songs and practising new ones in the music room with Steph and Michelle during our lunch breaks, or at athletics practice or playing goalkeeper for the school hockey team. I worked hard and was a bright and able student with a passion for biology and anything medical or scientific.

Our home was always filled with light and mum used to make sure that every evening we sat down together to have an evening meal, exchanging events of the day and discussing anything important or any outstanding issues. Often though we would just tell funny stories and our table would be filled with the sound of laughter.

Steph and I were now sleeping in separate bedrooms, but often moved into each other's room for the night as we missed each other or we needed to put the world to rights. We were best friends and soul mates. I loved and protected her and needed her confidence and carefree outlook to get me through my insecurities. I admired her wit and humour, her ability to have such positive faith in herself. I was so proud of her talents and silently tried to be like her. She was beautiful and petite and everyone that met her fell in love with her.

Joanne was my charge. I taught her to read and learn her numbers and colours; I bathed her and read her bedtime stories. She used to sit outside the toilet door waiting for me and she adored me unconditionally and totally, and I loved her as if she were not my sister but my child.

Our summers were spent on the beach rain or shine, and with friends that had holiday homes in the area. It was during one of the summers that Stephanie had her first true love experience, holding hands under the sand and gazing lovingly into his eyes. And at the same time I had a mini romance where I experienced my first compromising situation when the boy in question took me up to his hotel room and undid the first three buttons of my shirt. I enjoyed the thrill but wouldn't let him undo the rest!

During the winter months we would go to our local youth club on the weekend, or go out for hot chocolate and whipped cream in town. Wherever I went with Michelle and Stephanie we used to sing. Our guitars were always on our backs and we were constantly writing and practising and updating our repertoire, working on our harmonies and taking it all very seriously indeed.

There were actually four of us in the same year group; Sharon and Tracy were also part of our little clique. Although they were not involved with Triangle, they were an enormous part of my life.

Often on a Saturday night I would go to Tracy's flat and we would make pizza and spend our evening watching movies, doing our nails and hair and having heart-to-heart talks about the complexities of our lives that really did seem so complex at the time.

Sharon's life was very different from ours. She was the youngest of four children and her siblings were all very much older than her, which made her a great deal more independent than I was at the time. Michelle and I used to go to Sharon's house occasionally, but she had cats and we were both asthmatic and very allergic to cats so would spend our time there coughing, wheezing, sneezing and rubbing at our very puffed up eyes.

The three of us, however, spent many hours discussing how it would be for us when we were to become women. We compared our ripening bodies, conferred about our secret fantasies and occasionally acted them out. We practised our kissing skills and walked up and down the hallway trying to develop a sexy walk.

When we weren't trying to become sex symbols we would ride our bikes along the seafront to Beechy Head, pretending to be Steve Austin the Bionic Man, whom I was head over heels and hopelessly in love with.

We were living in our childish fantasy world, but balancing on the edge of womanhood, not quite sure which world we wanted more.

It really wasn't our choice to make. Slowly the bionic man was pushed to the back of my mind or in fact out of my head completely, and real boys who were more tangible but just as far out of reach replaced him.

I don't remember the first time I met David. He was much older than me. He was more of a man than any of the boys I had encountered at the local youth club, and he was already driving and had his own car. I am not quite sure why he was remotely interested in spending time with us, but I suspected at the time that he may have been in love with Stephanie; nevertheless he was suddenly in my house a lot and I was often in his. It eventually became more apparent that he was more interested in spending time with me, quite the mystery!

David was a very talented musician and wrote very insightful songs that he would perform to Michelle and me. We would often sit in his room starry eyed and feeling extremely mature nodding our approval, honoured and privileged that we were the ones chosen to be his critics and audience.

Just before my fourteenth birthday I went to London to celebrate my cousin Denise's engagement. We stayed in Redbridge in Essex with my grandparents. I was feeling quite unwell throughout the weekend, but not bad enough not to notice Denise's future brother-in-law Russell. We chatted shyly for a while and then lo and behold he actually asked me to dance. Me! The ugly duckling, the lanky, awkward, clumsy girl in the corner. I wasn't really sure what I was meant to do; I had never been in this situation. I tried to remember the scenarios that Michelle, Sharon and I had acted out, but none of them seemed appropriate for this moment. I had to rely on gut instinct. Thankfully it was a slow dance so I wouldn't have to exhibit my lack of co-ordination and rhythm on the dance floor. I put both my hands on his shoulders and moved my hips at least a foot away from his and prayed that I wouldn't step on his toes. It was surprisingly successful; we both survived our first dance and he even hung around to speak to me some more.

The evening flew by and I still had a pain in my stomach, even though I tried to ignore it and will it away. It was actually becoming harder to stand upright. Russell took my number before I left and he promised to call. I was not optimistic on that score!

The next day the ache in my stomach was still there and I was unable to function normally. So much so that my mother, who usually ignored any aches and pains we might have, actually showed concern and it seemed that she might well have been a touch worried. As the day progressed I was clearly in a great deal of discomfort so my parents took me to A&E. After horrendous examinations, which left me with zero dignity, and blood tests and countless hands prodding and pushing in all different directions, it was decided that I had appendicitis, so out it came.

The week I spent in hospital was atrocious. I was put in a post-op ward where the average age was eighty-five and the nurses tried to feed me semolina, custard and rice pudding; it was enough to put the pain right back in my stomach. Visiting time was limited and I was not allowed to wash my hair. It didn't do much for the image especially as I needed all the help I could get anyway.

The day before I was to be released I was lying on my bed reading yet another book when shockingly in walked Russell. What I felt at that moment is almost indescribable. It was delight that he felt he wanted to see me again, and then complete despair at the thought of what I must look like. I was sure at that moment that this would be our final meeting. I miraculously was wrong; he not only wanted to see me again, but he was taking me to the theatre in London. Just the two of us. Now I knew that I was no longer the bionic woman or man for that matter, I was becoming a real woman with a real date and even looking the way I did with my greasy hair, dark circles under my eyes and my winceyette pyjamas, he still wanted to take me out.

The only problem was with all of this, however flattering it was, was that I think I was in love with David Wayne, because he just kept popping into my head at the most inopportune moments. I wondered if perhaps it was possible to be in love with two people at the same time. I buried the thought and continued with the romance as planned.

Russell took me to see Elvis. We had a lovely evening, but I felt like a little girl (which I was) playing mums and dads. Conversation was a little disjointed and he never really knew what to do with his hands and I certainly had no idea. It was our first and final date!

Back in Bournemouth, David took me out for dinner. He collected me in his car and we went to an Italian restaurant for pizza. We spoke about concerts and moonlit walks and he said he would take me horse riding in the Isle of Wight (we never did do that). I was mesmerised, flattered, excited and scared all at the same time. What was this guy doing with me? I was just me, what on earth could he find that would appeal to him? Life was a conundrum and it just kept on surprising me. David was a true gentleman, or he was very aware that I was in fact considerably younger than him. He stopped on the way to show me a view from a desolated road in the middle of nowhere. I was a little uneasy and it crossed my mind that I wouldn't know what to do if he tried anything, but he didn't.

A few nights later David was at our house and had brought over the record of Paganini's Variations by Andrew Lloyd Webber for me to listen to for the first time. As it played the snow began to fall outside so fast and thick that it settled on the ground in minutes. David turned off all the lights and we stood the three of us, David, Steph and me, looking out of the window as the world became a winter wonderland, music blaring through the speakers as the snow fell to the melody. It was as if the night had been orchestrated just for us, just for this moment. It was a moment that made the world stand still; it was pure, innocent, clean and extremely romantic. It was a moment in time that will always remain one of my fondest.

One Saturday afternoon Michelle dragged me to a local hotel where a group of out of towners were staying as part of a youth weekend. It was here that I met Martin. He seemed much older than us and was quite uncouth and very loud. He had a Brighton and Hove Albion scarf tied around his wrist and a cigarette hanging from his mouth. He asked if Michelle and I would like to go down the pub later, but seemed a little put off when I replied that I would have to ask my father first. We didn't go to the pub and I soon put the rather shocking experience to the back of my mind. Martin later went out with a girl from Bournemouth who was somewhat more experienced than me in the boyfriend physical relationship department.

Suddenly our happy hazy summers and our cosy coddled winters ended. Dad was offered another promotion and once again we had to relocate. This time we were off to Brighton, another seaside town, but much more sophisticated and much less rural.

I had to leave my life of snowflakes and music, of hot chocolate and tree-lined roads. My friendships and first loves. All my wonderful firsts were here in this place. The thrill of new things excited me, yet the thought of all that I had to leave tormented me.

Off we went to try to find a home and whilst it seemed we were embarking on yet another adventure the timing was not great. I was in the middle of my O level syllabus and was on track to do medicine. My teachers were sure that I had the ability to pursue that avenue and I never doubted myself. It was my dream to become a doctor, not like Stephanie and Michelle who wanted to become famous. So the move to Brighton was not the most positive of choices as far as my future dreams were concerned.

Leaving the idyllic life that I had been living the last three and a half years was extremely heart-rending. It seemed I was leaving a secure, safe and protected world and embarking on a journey where I would have to use all of my emotional strengths and resources to cope with the enormous changes that were about to commence.

For a child of fourteen looking back now, that was a great deal to expect.

CHAPTER 3

Once more Brighton seemed like a completely different world. It's amazing how each move was so entirely dissimilar to the one before. Brighton was nowhere near as attractive or tranquil as Bournemouth, but still had some beautiful buildings, scenery and charm.

We had to rent a two-bedroomed flat when we arrived, because my parents hadn't found somewhere suitable to live.

School was a nightmare. The entire O level syllabuses were a different board, which meant that I had to start over again and complete the new syllabus in a year. Added to this, no schools in the area were able to offer me all my subjects, so I had to go to different schools for different subjects, and had to miss half chemistry in order to do half physics. It was all a bit of a disaster and eventually my form teacher was so confused as to where I was supposed to be and when that he told me to sign myself in the register at the end of every week!

The school that I was doing most of my lessons in was once again a mixed comprehensive and once more school became a rather unpleasant experience.

We joined the local synagogue and the youth club in the area, and who should I bump into, but Martin. Still with a cigarette hanging from his mouth, and his beat-up leather jacket, extremely tight jeans and his Brighton and Hove Albion scarf either round his neck or around his wrist. I am not actually quite sure why, but he took Stephanie and I under his wing and soon became a really good friend.

My parents eventually bought an old six-bedroomed house that needed to be completely renovated. It had a huge garden with an apple orchard in the back and beautiful pathways and features. Stephanie and I would walk there in our lunch break and sit in the garden eating the apples from the trees, imagining that we were happy and that we wouldn't have to return to the hell hole called school after we had eaten the apples.

Martin became a regular feature and he introduced me to plenty of people. I met another Michelle at a party and after two or three meetings we bumped into each other at the King Alfred swimming pool. After I had recovered from the shock that this girl, who was kind of the leader of the pack, wanted to talk to me, we began chatting and actually arranged to see each other the following weekend. It was the beginning of a friendship that would go on till this day.

Our rented flat overlooked the Sussex Cricket Ground, so often my newfound friends (who were informed by Martin about the wonderful views from our lounge window) would come and watch cricket matches. It was a blessing really because it meant that I could develop my confidence in my own surroundings and I began to grow and became a little less inhibited.

I fell in love with Russell. He was tall dark and handsome with jet-black hair that used to fall in his eyes when he danced. He was kind and funny and he filled my every thought. When I went to sleep the last face I saw was his, my heart would skip ten beats when he walked into the room, and if he brushed past me the point of contact would feel like it were on fire. I was completely and totally obsessed with him, praying and willing for him to like me the same way I did. I almost resorted to wishing on the first star, but I knew in my heart of hearts (just like I knew all those years ago) that it was an impossibility. I was known as the shy, innocent girl from some far off place, with no confidence and not particularly exciting either to look at or to talk to and certainly not very sexy. Russell was out of reach. I would never be able to change his mind.

Martin would call me every day promising to marry me one day. At the time he had a girlfriend that he quite liked and who liked him a lot. But even though she had a double barrelled name, she was not of the same religion so it would have to end otherwise he ran the risk of being excommunicated from his family. I had no romantic inclinations towards

Martin, he was just my best mate, so when he spoke of marrying me I would play along with his little game knowing that I would much rather that it were Russell asking for my hand.

In the absence of the third member of Triangle, Stephanie and I started singing without her. We soon became known, and sang several numbers in the community talent shows. We entered several competitions and Martin and Michelle became our faithful and loyal groupies.

One day whilst on the phone to Michelle I confessed my secret crush on Russell. In what I would soon learn was true Michelle style, she took over the situation and told me that in order to rid myself of my straight, frigid, girl from the country image I would have to go out with someone else first and at least get to second base (I pretended to know what second base was but in actual fact I didn't have a clue).

So it was decided. Martin was the obvious candidate; after all he was always declaring his love for me and informing me that one day I would be his wife. I later found out he was more attracted to the prospect of fine cuisine, the likes of which was served by my mother, than the attraction of myself. I am sure he did quite like me nevertheless as he was extremely tactile and very attentive. He spent more time in my home than his own and he was always there for meal times.

On 16th November 1978 we went to a disco at the youth club. Martin asked me to dance to "Lucky Stars" and as we danced he kissed me. It was a full-blown open-mouthed kiss with tongues. Amazingly, it didn't cause the same response as my first French kiss. I actually enjoyed it! There were strange sensations in my tummy and my body trembled with excitement. I was certainly not expecting this reaction. I thought about the plan and realised it may have just been foiled.

Many years later I found out that at the same time Martin walked over to ask me to dance Russell was walking over to do the same. It seems he got pipped to the post!

CHAPTER 4

My friendship with Martin didn't really change; we had been more or less inseparable anyway. Now we just added some kissing and groping. Actually, Martin couldn't get enough kissing and groping. He wanted to kiss and cuddle on every street corner, every alley and every lamppost. It was a tad embarrassing, but I just thought that I had better go along with it, as I didn't really want to live up to my reputation.

My family eventually moved into our new house and I remembered the concept of space. The house was enormous, with six bedrooms, a music room and ironing room, basements and cellars. It was the kind of house that you could lose yourself in. It was full of nooks and crannies and it seemed that if it could speak it would tell a thousand stories.

School continued to be ghastly, but now that I had Martin as my boyfriend, Michelle as my friend and Stephanie as my soul mate, work suddenly didn't seem so important. Not only that I was more or less a free agent. My main school didn't really know where I was supposed to be and had given me permission to come and go as I pleased, so as you can imagine I weighed up the options and decided that it was much more important to have some fun.

Martin introduced me to the joys of smoking and I was beginning to enjoy the effects of alcohol. We used to have a regular Tuesday morning meet where Michelle, Martin and I would sit around the breakfast table smoking and drinking gin and tonics, after which we would attempt to go back to school for a few hours in the afternoon, but not enough to gain success in any of our exams. Consequently, medicine was no longer an option, although I do believe it no longer became an option the day we moved away from Bournemouth.

The seasons changed and as our exams loomed nearer I became less and less enthusiastic about my books and more and more interested in my body. I used to be sent to my room to revise, where I gazed aimlessly at my ill-written half missing notes. It would be like trying to put together a jigsaw that had lost half the pieces. My eyes skimmed the pages, but my mind was thinking about Martin's hands exploring the space between my very ill-fitting bra that was miles too big and my breasts that sat tiny and pert underneath. I don't remember feeling earth shatteringly excited by it all, but more curious and inquisitive into what would happen next and eager to find out about the next instalment. Martin was still rather clumsy and inexperienced but was determined to keep rehearsing, and he really liked to rehearse a great deal.

He was leaving for Camp America for the summer and was leaving straight after exams. He was to be away for three months; the thought of it reduced us both to tears on several occasions. That amount of time at that age seemed like an eternity, and we could not imagine that the summer would ever be over. To be apart for that length of time having spent so much time together over the last eight months was almost unthinkable. I, however, did handle it slightly better than him!

I was now working part time in a Rock Shop on Brighton Beach. Stephanie and I job shared or when the shop was busy we would work together. It was generally just the two of us in the shop, the owners would pop in and out, but we were generally left to our own devices. It was immense fun. All the roller skaters and guys on rollerblades used to come in for Mr Whippy ice creams, and in our lunch hour Stephanie would drag me along to the skateboard park so she could look lovingly and ever hopefully at the long-haired, bronzed, beautiful-bodied skateboarder that she was hopelessly in love with.

I had improved my image a little by that summer and having a boyfriend did wonders for my self-confidence. So I used to flirt with the boys from what seemed to be a very safe distance.

The night Martin left for America we partied hard then woke up extremely early, and I went with him to the airport. Martin had had an argument with his parents about something that he was not prepared to talk

about, but I suspected it may have something to do with our relationship and the fact that they didn't really approve of the two of us being together. His eyes were bleary and tear-stained and he was a little distracted. We did the usual photo booth picture and the exceptionally dramatic "I love you" and major snogging as we said goodbye at passport control, and then he went his way and I left to go home.

By the time I arrived home I had gathered myself together and had resigned myself to a summer without Martin. I had my job, and loads of friends and was off camping with mum and dad for two weeks, so I was quite happy for my summer to begin. I was sixteen and having fun, who knew what might happen.

Mum told me to call his mother when I arrived home, because she said it would be a kind thing to do, to tell her that her son had arrived at the airport safely. So being the lovely dutiful person that I was, I called her. BIG MISTAKE! She hurled abuse down the phone, about what a disgusting, badly brought up, disrespectful person I was. How I had led her son astray and that my parents should be ashamed of themselves for letting our relationship continue for as long as it had, and other more horrendous slanderous comments. There was no response, I couldn't actually form any words, I searched in my head for something to say that may resolve the situation but there was just no reply. It was like listening to someone so irrational and unhinged that whatever I might have thought about saying would actually have been a complete waste of breath. I numbly gave the phone to my mum who was now standing next to me listening, head next to mine, to the receiver. I don't remember what was said after that, but that day sealed my fate.

No one was going to tell me I couldn't have something unless I didn't want it too, and at that moment I wanted a relationship. Now that it was not going to be an easy ride, the thought and excitement of the challenge was enough to make me more determined.

CHAPTER 5

Soon after Martin left for America and after I had completed all my O Level exams, the summer students from abroad arrived in Brighton determined to learn how to speak English in six weeks. The town was buzzing. The Rock Shop was busy all day; I think I may have held the record for the most Mr Whippy ice creams pulled!

A boy called Frederick from France came to the shop everyday and every day he asked me to go out for coffee with him. Each time I declined, but he was persistent even with the knowledge that I had a boyfriend. After he promised that he would behave appropriately I agreed to go out with him for the evening. After all I was sure that however much Martin missed me he was not going to avoid speaking to other girls. As it turned out, many years later I found out that he was doing a lot more than chatting to other girls whilst he was away.

Anyway, back on track. Frederick took me to a club. We actually had a really lovely evening and when he said goodbye he made me promise to call him should my relationship ever come to an end. I wonder if he is still waiting!

When I went home that night I wrote Martin yet another letter. The distance between us seemed so vast. I really missed him, but part of me wanted to pretend that he didn't exist and just have the sort of fun a sixteen-year-old should be having. Brighton was heaving and the world should have been my oyster, but I loved my boyfriend and didn't think I would be able to live with the guilt if I were to be unfaithful. If only I could have seen across the water.

So the summer passed. I worked every day at the shop with the exception of a two-week break to go camping with my parents and sister Joanne, which was an experience to behold!

We went to the Lake District and slept in a deluxe tent, which we trailed on the back of the car; something my dad had no experience in. Turning corners and three point turns was a little bit challenging! It did not stop raining for the whole two weeks that we were away. There was no one else to talk to, just the four of us, and Joanne was only eight and as much as I loved her she was not so great at the relationship advice. Mum and dad were fantastic to be with and we enjoyed each other's company, except when she insisted on nagging him about the most inane things. Occasionally he would snap back and there would be a minor war for a few hours, but eventually harmony would be restored and we would continue with our holiday on an even keel. I was not best impressed with the communal showers or having to trek across fields if I needed the toilet in the middle of the night. It was, however, a great source of amusement and we laughed at the situation as opposed to crying.

Stephanie had saved enough money to go to stay with our Aunty Gloria and Uncle Harry, my dad's sister and brother-in-law in America, and she was planning on speaking to Martin whilst she was out there.

When our holiday finally came to an end, I returned home to fourteen letters from Martin on the door mat expressing his love for me and saying how much he missed me and that he couldn't wait to be home with me again. Also on the mat were my O level results which were not so wonderful. I had only passed English Language which required no revision and had failed all the others. Oh dear, it looked like it was to be Sixth Form College for retakes come September.

Martin's results were not much better. His parents were not happy and completely blamed his bad performance on our relationship. They were probably right. His father flew to America to try and persuade him to finish with me on his return, but he was having none of that. The more resistance his parents put up, the more determined we became to stay together. It was becoming a battle of wills. The only problem, and it was quite a huge problem, was that whilst I remained rational throughout, Martin was not coping so well with the pressure. His determination to be with me never faltered, but he was not able to focus and seemed to be distracted and distant. This was all going on whilst he was away, but he started to call me every other day and the content of the call was becoming less rational and the urgency in his voice for reassurance was tangible. He was supposed to be travelling around America when he had finished camp, but he completely shut down and began to emotionally crumble. So my wonderful uncle travelled two hundred miles to collect him and bring him back to Rhode Island.

They were amazing to him, they fed him up and gave him a bed and security then looked after him until he was ready to go home. Heaven knows what they must have thought. This was the boy I was telling them I was so much in love with and he was a wreck, but they never once said that they didn't approve.

Stephanie on her return to England had fallen in love with Aunty Gloria's stepson Keith. She could talk about nothing else, how he taught her how to smoke, drink and other things. She did remember to tell me about how dreadful Martin had been and how disturbing it had been to see him in such a bad way. She said that he was completely messed up and she thought that he might have been having a breakdown. I took on board her warnings and buried them deep, deep in the crevices of my memory bank for use at a future date and then I endeavoured to continue with what was proving to be anything but a straight forward relationship.

Looking back now I truly believe that had we been left alone and had Martin been left to pick up his pieces without immense pressure from his parents, the chances are we would have fizzled out. He would have moved to London and I would have done something in Brighton, and I would have tired of a long distance normal relationship and would have wanted to move onto something more exciting. This way I had everything. I had challenging, exciting, out of the ordinary, and never for one minute mundane.

Martin's father took him all around the country looking for courses that he could access with the results that he didn't achieve. I think they really wanted him as far away from me as possible (another challenge). He eventually enrolled into North London Polytechnic to study a diploma in Business, whilst I enrolled at the local sixth form college, which was just a ten-minute walk up the road from my house.

He went off to college in London and found some dreadful digs to live in and I embarked on yet another adventure, sixth form! I really loved the social life there. I had loads of friends, mostly boys as I always seemed to relate better to them; they didn't make me feel quite so inhibited and they didn't want to compete with anything that I may or may not do. Relationships with boys as friends I have always found to be far less complicated, it's always just what it is with no hidden agendas. I did, however, make friends with one girl, Alison, who became a really close friend. She was absolutely beautiful with the longest legs I had ever seen, perfect features and blonde hair and blue eyes, something I had always yearned to have. We became good friends early into our time at college probably because we were both in steady relationships and that was quite unusual. The only difference between her steady relationship and mine was that she was living with her much older boyfriend and I was having a long distance relationship.

Our friendship was cemented one month when we both discovered our periods were late. In a panic we both called the abortion clinic. Her financial situation was better than mine in that her boyfriend was able to fund what ever needed to be done, whilst we couldn't. We had to call Martin's friend Paul and put him on hold for a potential loan. I don't think he was very impressed with us at that moment.

As it turned out the panic had been futile as I started my period a week later. I did lose a couple of pounds in weight as a result of the stress all the worry had caused, so out of bad does come good or so I thought.

There were a few more similar scares through the years, but none had to ever be addressed in the end. Later I would reflect on those times and it all made sense.

My studies at college continued pretty much in the same vein as they had in school, lots of socialising and not so much studying. Mum had commandeered a student from Sussex University called Julian to tutor me in maths. He became a regular fixture in our home and miraculously he did get me through the exam and I passed with a C, and we had so much fun in the process. Water fights, play fights (I always ended up underneath him), rides in the car, coffees and meals out, but we were just friends.

My social life started to become a bit diverse. I spent a great deal of time with Ali and Dave (her thirty-four-year-old boyfriend). Their life was so far removed from anything I had ever known and I was completely in awe of it and desperately wanted to be part of it. I loved different, and this was. They had their own flat and a boat, and he used to take me trout fishing. He introduced me to the evil weed and I loved it, and he really liked younger girls. That guilt thing that I was so worried about in the summer wasn't so bad after all!

I always think of this time as my time of rebellion and if that was as bad as it became then I was actually not so terrible. The worst thing that I did was smoke a little marijuana and was a little promiscuous. I did eventually come out the other end and no one knew or suffered as a result.

CHAPTER 6

After a year at college, some wild parties, and plenty of drinking and smoking, I ended up with Biology, English and Maths O levels, on top of my English Language exam that I had achieved at my last school, so although I was never going to be a high flying graduate or a doctor for that matter, I had four reasonably respectable results.

I decided that my days in the Rock Shop must come to an end and it was time to make some proper considerations into the type of career I might want to pursue. I had no interest in sitting behind a word processor, taking notes and being told what to write, who to write it for, when and how, so any secretarial role for me was out of the question. As mentioned earlier, a career in medicine, which was my one true dream, was no longer a possibility, which left teaching or some sort of related profession. I had not achieved the grades to go on to do A levels, so university was not an option. Besides which I had no intention of moving away from Martin; life was much too exciting with him to walk away from it!

So I went to work in the Jewish kindergarten which coincidentally was run by my mother. Well, it takes a certain type of person to work with a parent or a child for that matter, but somehow we managed to separate our working lives from our home lives and actually mum was an extremely proficient teacher. I learnt my trade well and also became quite competent at my job. I loved the satisfaction of moulding these tiny minds so hungry for knowledge and the trust and love that they bestowed upon me that was unconditional. How one week they were unable to recognise the colour red and then because of something that I had said or done they then knew red, blue and green.

I found it so incredible how their learning experience became mine also. How their quest for knowledge opened up gates into my mind that had until then remained closed. My job was satisfying and fulfilling, but I was earning dreadful money. Not only that, but I finished work at three o' clock every day and that felt like lunch time.

I decided to entirely split my day and work mornings as a nursery school teacher and afternoons as a dental nurse, working for the friend of the family whose practice was only a few doors down from the kindergarten.

I went to college in Lewis one day a week to do a preschool playgroup certificate and went one evening a week to Brighton College to do a certificate in dental nursing. Throughout all of this I was still enjoying an extremely active social life. Most Saturday nights I would go to the local night club and most Sundays I spent nursing a hangover. I was a typical teenager!

My mum taught me to drive and I eventually passed after my second attempt and life at that time seemed free and dandy.

Martin was back and forth at weekends and often I would go to London. The majority of his studying took place in the snooker hall of his college and I think his books rarely made an appearance, but he was having plenty of fun: smoking packet loads of cigarettes, consuming large amounts of alcohol, lots of poker, snooker and partying and not an awful lot of studying.

Stephanie was dating a really lovely boy who she once again was madly in love with. Unfortunately, my parents were not happy with this little liaison as Bradley was not of the same faith and although both Steph and Bradley were extremely young and merely having a good time exploring the realms of teenage sexuality, my parents panicked and sent Stephanie packing off to London to try and find something that may complete her there.

All she wanted to do was to act and have a boyfriend of any denomination and all they wanted her to do was have a nice job and a nice "Jewish boyfriend" preferably a doctor or solicitor!

So I was left at home under mum and dad's roof, with Joanne still my sidekick and Martin away in London commuting backwards and forwards when it suited him.

Stephanie leaving changed our home and of course my life. The two of us up to this point had been so completely intertwined. I had always been her confidante, and to a certain extent her mine, although I was never quite as open and happy to vocalise my emotions as readily as Stephanie did. For her I was practical support, helping to rationalise so many of her uncertainties, whereas she was for me a silent reinforcement. I didn't need to speak for her to know if I was concerned or distressed about something, and although she probably wasn't even aware of it, her mere presence often gave me the reassurance and confidence I so often needed. So when she was no longer living with me under the same roof it felt like a loss. I felt I had mislaid an important part of my person and a little fragment of a space inside my heart felt empty and alone.

Stephanie ended up living in all sorts of not very salubrious dwellings and tried her hand at a selection of varying places of employment, none of which she was very impressed or enamoured with. Eventually she auditioned for drama school and managed to ensure a place.

In the meantime Bradley would wait for me outside Brighton College every week looking for ways back into Stephanie's life, and whilst she was still interested in having his attentions I think it was more to feed her ego than to share his love.

I missed Stephanie in my life as a constant, but I think this period was our most separate. It was during this time that our lives went in very different ways. She outgrew her suburban, closeted life and went to explore pastures greener in the form of drama students, drugs and rock n roll, whilst I followed my little path of very quiet rebellion, chicken soup and socialising.

By the time I was eighteen Martin and I decided to make our relationship official. He never really asked me to marry him; it was just assumed that I would.

His parents wanted to make it as difficult as possible for us and tried to put as many obstacles in our way as possible, but during the inquisition (which was supposed to be our wonderful joyous engagement announcement) we calmly pointed out, as we were hauled separately into the question box, that we were both in fact over eighteen and that if we wanted to we could marry without both their permission and their blessing, and we were quite prepared to do this if they were to continue to make things difficult for us. They had no choice, we agreed not to marry for a further two years and they agreed to give us their blessing.

One–Nil to me! In my head they had lost that round miserably. They were as happy about our union as they would have been if I had announced that I had a terminal illness, actually they probably would have preferred that scenario!

How short sighted I was and naïve. It was all a game of who would get the prize and in hindsight there could be no winners at all; but they threw down the gauntlet and I had to take the challenge and fight back.

There were many ups and downs and small emotional rollercoaster rides during the period of our engagement, but none monumental and significant enough to recollect.

Wedding plans began to take place. My parents took on board my intentions and never once questioned the sensibility of what I was taking on, or the possibility that I may not be emotionally equipped to deal with the enormity of marrying a person like Martin and the baggage that he inherited as a result of his upbringing. I sometimes wish now that they had been more insightful and more opinionated, but in reality it would have just become another challenge and the result would have still been the same but with a little more bad blood.

So they took on the arrangements with gusto and enthusiasm, and being popular members of the community it was to become a society event. It was the talk of the town and there really was no backing down.

By this time Alison and Dave had split up and gone their separate ways, but I was still friendly with both of them. Dave emigrated to Australia in the January before my wedding and his parting words to me were "DON'T DO IT!"

I didn't listen and on 8th April 1984 we were married in Middle Street Synagogue in Brighton, followed by a massive party hosting 270 people at the Hove Town Hall.

Here began the next chapter of my life.

CHAPTER 7

April 1984. Our wedding day was pretty normal; I looked beautiful, even though I had decided two weeks before my wedding that I didn't like my dress! My husband looked at me through loving, young hopeful eyes. We were full of youthful ambition, our future was our own, and we could do with it what we wanted. We were the new Mr and Mrs Martin Lerner and we were going to do everything right.

Our honeymoon was to the Canary Islands and we spent our days making love, drinking, holding hands and flirting with the other couple that we had befriended. Martin burnt and spent the first couple of days complaining about how sensitive his skin was feeling, and although it made some of our activities a little more complicated somehow we managed to find ways around that problem.

Our holiday ended after a week, although I felt as though it was only about to begin. I was beside myself with excitement waiting to return to our flat, with everything new, even the freshly painted walls that we had spent hours perfecting together, and the big drips of gloss on the doors that was a memento of Martin's impatience and insistence on using a big paint brush instead of a small one to ensure smoothness.

I was eager to embark on the adventures of domesticity, of moving out of my family home and knowing that this new home was my domain and I was no longer answerable to my parents. The only person who now had control over me was my husband, and at the time I was happy with that, although I am sure that I didn't perceive it as him having control over me.

I remember lying in the bath on that first day home after we had returned from our honeymoon, my skin glowing with sun kissed shine, looking around and thinking to myself that this was mine, my very own home, everything in it belonged to me and of course Martin, but the kitchen was now my domain; if I wanted to leave the dishes unwashed in the sink no one would or could tell me to wash them or clean up. I felt free and euphoric; the anticipation of what lay ahead was almost too much to bear.

We did not consider that certain aspects of life were beyond our control. So when after a few months we decided to try for a family, we were filled with all the excitement and dreams that all young couples have when embarking on their journey into parenthood.

Martin had gone to work for a firm of chartered accountants before we were married with a view to studying and qualifying, as his father had done, to become a chartered accountant. He found revising impossible and soon decided that this was not an avenue that he was likely to be successful in. He was driven by success and making money and also by status, he was always striving to be better than the next person to show the world that he would and could make it and become a respected and accomplished business man; this was not only his ambition it was his obsession. If you look long and hard enough it is always possible to find an opportunity, and one eventually presented itself in the form of John Tobin. He was a client of the firm where Martin was articled. He was a big property investor and worked from offices in Sloane Street in Knightsbridge. Martin impressed him with his knowledge and ability to retain and rationalise information about property and investment and he soon became John's right hand man.

The time to think about expanding our family was right; Martin gave the idea the go ahead. I no longer walked through the park looking at the autumn trees, or smelling the freshly cut grass, nor even did I notice the bed of newly flowering autumn posies. No, I was now looking at the little baby sucking its toes, or the pregnant lady, waddling slightly in those rather fetching maternity dungarees, and I thought to myself soon it will be my turn. Soon I can waddle slowly through the park, planning my special day, wondering if it will be a girl or boy, who would it look like, and dreams and scenarios of a similar kind. Everything took on a different meaning.

Sex was no longer an act of love it became an act of procreation. Will this be it? Have we made a baby this time?

I used to lie in bed imagining the hundreds and thousands of little sperm making their way up to the egg, waiting expectantly for their arrival. Which one would get there first, would it be a boy sperm or a girl sperm, or perhaps twins?

My flat suddenly was no longer the party pad it had been up until now. The spare room would make such a beautiful nursery, but would there be room in our lounge area for all of the baby's paraphernalia?

So parenthood suddenly became my life. Nothing was as important any more. It wasn't long before our closest friends announced that they were soon to be parents, and as expected my excitement grew, and consequently the questions began. How long had they been trying? Was it better on your back, front, legs up or legs down? What time of the month? And so on and so forth. But even having gathered all the relevant information, and apparently doing everything correctly, after six months we were no nearer to becoming three.

So we bought a puppy. Maybe she would alleviate some of the pressure, curb my maternal instincts for a while and ease that anxiety, and with some of the pressure off I would more than likely fall pregnant.

Martin had begun to work for John and commuting everyday to London. We started socialising with a crowd of people who were much older than ourselves and a great deal more established then we were. Often we had to decline dinner invitations with them because we couldn't make our finances stretch that far.

It didn't detract from the fact that I was determined to have a baby even if I had to make half a pound of mince meat go for four meals!

Most weekends and often during the week we would be out drinking and having a rather wild time. Our new friends enjoyed our youthful energy and the fact that our lives were without the same commitments as their own. When we returned to our flat, heads whirling and high from dope and drink, we would make love with an urgency that was not about passion and love but about function and determination. My goal was always there in the forefront of my mind and no amount of drink could numb that urgency. I was determined to become pregnant and surely that drive and persistence was enough.

Fate, however, had other ideas. Some months later after the arrival of our dear friends' first child, I became impatient. Why wasn't I pregnant? There must be something not quite right. Not to worry I said to myself, nothing that can't be fixed. But somewhere deep, deep, in the pit of my stomach I wasn't so sure. Why was I feeling this rather uneasy stirring? Just an irrational stupid feeling. Suppress it because it won't help matters. And so I did.

CHAPTER 8

To be on the safe side and to put my very active mind at rest, I sought an opinion from a gynaecologist who had a local private practice in Hove (where we were currently living).

I must say I did feel somewhat of a fraud. After all, women tried for years before they admitted defeat, and here was I impatient and ready to try anything that would put an end to this empty yearning. It was almost as if I was on a mission and nothing was going to distract me, nothing at all.

Well I don't think Mr Masters took me very seriously. I remember the way he looked at me when I said that actually it wasn't even a year since I had started trying for a baby, and he said that perhaps if I just relaxed and didn't think about it quite so much ... but if I really was concerned I should go away and try some temperature charts, that should give us a much clearer picture of what was actually going on in my ovaries.

Oh, and of course we must do a sperm count on Martin, after all the problem (if there was one) may lie with him. Okay, now I had to go home and tell Martin that making love twice a day was not enough, now he was going to have to ejaculate into a bottle. Not only that, once he had, he had to take the bottle and its contents to the local Pathological Laboratory, which was run by someone we knew, and the receptionist also happened to be a friend of ours. Mmm, perhaps a bottle of wine and a box of his favourite chocolates were in order!

Being the wonderful person that he was, Martin said he would do anything that would make me happy, and of course there was absolutely no way that the problem could lie with him, but it would be a good idea to rule it out.

So early the next morning, bottle in hand, he tootled off to the bathroom. After a lot of huffing and puffing, oohing and ahhing, he screamed out for help, explaining in no uncertain terms that he could really use a hand or something.

How is it that men spend so much of there adult life managing quite expertly well on their own until they are under a little bit of pressure, and then they really need help. Not this time, this was one thing he was going to have to do alone, and he did.

I remember it was quite a warm day that day, and it was important that the sample in a bottle didn't reach a certain temperature, so he drove to the laboratory with all the windows open, praying quietly that there would be no traffic jams on the way. Luckily for him there wasn't, and he didn't stop to explain at reception, he just dropped the bottle and ran.

As usual he was right, his sperm count was fine, he was a perfect specimen of a man; the problem (if there was one) obviously lay with me. So we started the temperature charts. I went and bought a mercury thermometer, they didn't make digital in those days, digital watches were still a novelty, and with charts, thermometer and pen in hand I went to bed.

Well, to be perfectly honest my charts and temperature were a bit of a flat line. According to the sample charts they were supposed to go up and down at certain times of the month, and when my temperature dipped that was the time that I was more likely to fall pregnant, but my temperature never did dip. So I started hallucinating, and saying to myself that, oh yes, I had gone down a degree, now must be the right time. So out came the candles, and the smoochy music, and a few dirty magazines just to ensure that there was no room for mistakes or pressure droops! And then I would wait, and lo and behold, I always, always started my period right on time.

Then one day Martin came up with a brain wave. If we moved house we would have a different focus, maybe then things would happen. So our flat went on the market, and we found a rather large house that our puppy took great delight in chewing to bits.

Whilst all this was going on Martin's career was going from strength to strength. He was now trading with the big boys, dealing with hundreds of thousands of pounds. He took on the persona of a Sloane Ranger and his ego and self-esteem grew along with his bank account. The hours that he worked increased and he often returned home way after I had gone to sleep, but nevertheless would wake me in order to have sex, or make love however it is you want to look at it. I think that this was more to satisfy his needs as opposed to my need for becoming pregnant.

Our friends were not so interested in inviting me around to socialise without Martin, so I began spending a substantial time alone with my own anxieties trying to make sense of the way my life was changing. Actually, it wasn't so much my life that was changing it was more the way that I was viewing it.

By now it was the summer of 1985. We had been married just over a year. Instead of glowing with newlywed satisfaction I was becoming increasingly thinner. Our new house was the most uninviting, chewed up, dusty, half finished ram shack and I hated it, and to make matters worse he was never there. He began to work increasingly long hours, and I spent most evenings alone, dwelling on how unlucky I was, and how unfair my life was, because I wanted a baby and couldn't have one, and how my husband with the HUGE ego was becoming less and less interested in me and my thermometer, and even my eagerness for him in the bedroom didn't seem to excite him any longer. Life at this time was not good, and there didn't seem to be a light at the end of the tunnel.

CHAPTER 9

It continued on this path for a while, Martin never home, me completely obsessed with falling pregnant, our friends becoming more and more distant, and our house becoming more and more disorganised.

It was on a weekend in Bournemouth, at the wedding of an old friend, that we made a decision. And looking back I would say it was that decision that saved us (or not). The time had come to admit that if we carried on going on the present path we would eventually come to a crossroads and have to go our separate ways. So we once again put our house on the market, and went in search of our dreams in Elstree and Borehamwood.

Leaving Brighton where we had met, married and dated didn't create the sort of emotions that I had expected to feel. I think that it was perhaps because I had moved homes so often when growing up that I approached this new phase with excited expectation. I was filled with positive hope for a new beginning and was more than eager to leave the house that I had grown to hate.

Leaving mum and dad was going to be the biggest wrench, but even that didn't make me sad. I knew that they would always be there for me either on the end of a phone or on visits up and down the M23. Dad was used to travelling all over the country so sixty miles up the motorway was not a challenge for him.

Stephanie was already living in London so I would be able to re-establish our close alliance, and Joanne was busy with her friends creating havoc in her wake.

As for my friends! Well, my new friends promised to stay in touch declaring love and loyalty forever and my old friends knew that distance cannot weaken the ties of friendship, so we were certain to remain part of each other's lives always.

We started our new life in a very small, very pretty neo-Georgian terrace house. When I sat in my house on that first evening, I thought that I would never want to live anywhere else. It was a cold November day the day that we moved, and as the last box was delivered, and I closed our new front door and stepped into the sitting room, so perfectly decorated, with pale grey walls and pastel pink festooned curtains framing the tiny white Georgian bay windows, I knew that I had really come home this time, and I really believed that we would find the strength together to overcome any of the hurdles that may come our way. I was truly happy, and thought that I could never be anything else.

Life took on a different slant for a few months. I went to work for a dentist, who also became a friend, and Martin, although working very hard, came home for dinner most evenings. Our social life became very active, as did our sex lives. Although having a baby was still very much wanted, it was no longer right at the top of the list. We were actually having fun.

February 1986. It always amazes me that no matter how in control you believe you are, fate always has the upper hand. Fate is something we really don't have any control over. It was very cold that day in February. I went to work as usual, but my dog had been unwell, and I had to tell Colin (the dentist) that I would have to leave early to take her to the vet.

I remember on the way to work wondering when that pain in my side would subside. I thought that it was probably an ovulation pain, so tonight we were definitely on for a romantic evening in for two. The pain didn't go, but it wasn't unbearable, and I did manage to last the day, and I managed to eat my usual obscene amounts of food.

Martin arrived home shortly after I had returned from the vet. He was laden with a new television, plus a cabinet that was still flat packed. We exchanged events of the day, and although he acknowledged my niggling pain, he was much more interested in his new toys, and insisted that I should be his assistant in assembling them.

His lack of concern for my well being really infuriated me, so I complained a little louder, still no reaction. So I thought that I would show him once and for all that I was more important than a television, and I phoned the emergency doctor.

Well, things kind of happened rather quickly and extremely dramatically after that. I ended up in casualty, and they didn't know what was wrong with me. Then the questions started. Had we been trying for a baby, how long had we been trying, and when was my period due? With all these questions all I could think about was that I was trying to prove a point and was all this fuss a little extreme, and how could a little niggle possibly be anything serious. It was when they mentioned that there was a possibility that I might have an ectopic pregnancy, that I realised that even a little niggle could turn into a big pain. As it so happened I was becoming increasingly more uncomfortable, and sitting up was quite an effort. I had had enough of being in pain, I needed some pain relief, a couple of paracetamols would have done nicely, but oh no, this was the National Health Service so a pethidine shot was all that was on offer.

I really cannot remember exactly what happened after that, because my head was six feet higher than it usually was, and I found it very difficult to focus on what people were saying to me. I suddenly felt very tired and was unable to keep my eyes open for long periods of time, and my mouth seemed to be unable to move and make word sounds in the way that it normally did. I do remember feeling very cold as they wheeled me through the hospital corridors and very grateful when I was finally moved into a proper bed in a very dark ward.

During that first night the nurse, prodding and listening, woke me up regularly, but the night passed, and by morning I felt ready to go home. The doctors, however, had other ideas; they wanted to have a look inside to see what was going on. Now was the time I thought that perhaps we should phone mum, because I really needed her. There is no one better than your mum in a time of crisis. Husbands are not the same, and at that moment in time I needed my mum, but she lived in Brighton and the doctors were not wasting any time. They whisked me off to theatre, and my mum wasn't there to give me a cuddle. It was the first time since getting married that I felt that I was really only a vulnerable little girl, playing a grown up game, and I was really frightened.

Thankfully, it was not an ectopic pregnancy, my tubes were all intact, and they could see no reason why I was unable to conceive. The operation actually took two hours because I had a burst haematoma; as far as I am aware that is a big clot of blood that has burst. It had been caused by an ovarian cyst and they had to find all the little bits of blood, because otherwise one might find its way into an organ like the heart or lungs, and if that were to happen then there would be extremely serious consequences, i.e. death.

However, that had not happened, I had come through the operation safely, and when I woke, my mum was there to give me the hug that I so desperately needed, and Martin was there on the other side of the bed holding my hand, so all was well. Very soon we would be able to put this little episode behind us, and carry on having fun, or could we?

The feelings that were stirred in the knowledge that we thought that we had lost a baby were extremely mixed. If in fact I had had an ectopic pregnancy then at least I would know that I could fall pregnant. Then there was that feeling of grief, and loss and frustration that we felt for only a short time, but it was so overwhelming that once again we were struggling with a new range of emotions, and so our horizons had changed, and it was time to follow yet another new path.

CHAPTER 10

I spent a week recovering in hospital, and five weeks at home. It was then that I went for my six week post-operative check up. Mr Humand was the gynaecologist who had operated on me and effectively saved my life. I sat with him and explained at this appointment that I had been trying to fall pregnant for some time, and nothing seemed to be happening.

Mr Humand sent me home with a prescription for a drug called Clomid. It was supposed to regulate my periods and stimulate my ovaries. It also gives you hot flushes, and it made me quite bloated, but I did not worry about any of those things, help was at hand and I was grabbing it with both of mine.

Mr Humand said that he would see me again when I was either pregnant or when I needed another prescription. I must say that on reflection his bedside manner did leave a lot to be desired, but at the time I thought he was my Knight in Shining Armour, he was the man that was going to make me a mummy.

As always things did not go quite to plan, and after six months of hot flushes, I had had enough of Mr Humand and his ineffective Clomid. So I called my cousin, who had successfully come through the infertility circuit (albeit not without a lot of heartache), and she gave me the name of her endocrinologist.

Martin and I went together to see Dr Gayle. She was only about four foot ten, but she was extremely formidable, and quite scary. Poor Martin was not expecting to be examined, and when she demanded that he drop his trousers behind the screen so that she could inspect his testicles, his pallor went from healthily pink to deathly white. Still after what seemed to him like an eternity, she announced that his testicles seemed perfectly healthy, but another sperm test would be in order.

At that moment I felt sorry for Martin, having to endure the indignities of all that was going on, but in time I would come to realise that I would have gladly swapped places with him if it meant that that was ALL that I would have to endure.

Dr Gayle sent us both off for a series of blood tests and scans that were to take place over the course of a month, after which we were to return to discuss her findings and work out a plan of action.

I had never spent much time in the Harley Street area, but I was soon to know every secret parking space, short cut and taxi rank. After a month and with all our data collected we sat nervously in Dr Gayle's waiting room. Waiting was something that we were beginning to be good at. Was this the woman that would change our world? Once she had found the problem (if there was one), would she be able to help us? What did we really want her to tell us? What if she said that there was absolutely nothing wrong with either of us? We would then have to go away and keep trying, but we had already been trying for what seemed such a long time, and so the thoughts ran.

When she finally called us into her room, I felt almost relief when she turned round to me and explained in no uncertain terms that if I were to succeed in getting pregnant I would most definitely need dynamite.

I will never forget those words. They were the words that I thought I had wanted to hear for quite some time. But the reality was chilling. Knowing now that things were not in working order, how long would it take to correct that, had they invented a fertility drug that equated to dynamite?

Strangely, I felt quite calm. I didn't make a conscious decision about how I was going to approach this problem. I don't think that I was surprised with the results; I felt at the time that there was not enough information and I did not know how to source what I needed to know. It was some years before the internet would be at our disposal.

The thing about infertility is that it is not in our control. I felt that if I knew more I would be able to influence the end result. Rationally of course this was absurd, but I just needed to feel that I was being constructive as opposed to inactive.

Someone once said that ignorance is bliss. How true that was in that moment, for if we had had the knowledge of what lay ahead, would we have chosen to stay on the same path?

Dr Gayle then explained the course of action that she thought would achieve the desired effect, and consequently result in a baby at the end. I was to start on a drug called Pergonal. This could be administered in varying strengths, and she would start me on a medium strength of four ampoules every day for fourteen to sixteen days, starting on the first day of my period. During that time I would have to come to Harley Street at least twice a week for a scan and a blood test, possibly more. Pergonal is a drug that stimulates the ovaries to produce more than one egg. It is the drug that was given to both the Waltons and the Colemans and they ended up with sextuplets. Once the scan showed that my eggs were ready and ripe she would give me another drug called HCG which is a drug that releases the eggs into the Fallopian tubes, where one or perhaps more will meet a sperm and become an embryo. Simple as that!

Oh, one more very important factor, these drugs were administered by injection, and they had to be given at the correct time on the correct day, and it was my job to organise that with my GP. Trying to persuade a doctor's secretary that I needed to make an appointment on a definite day at a definite time would prove to be quite a challenge, but I suppose this was God's way of keeping me busy.

When we left Dr Gayle's rooms we were a little shell shocked. We were about to embark on a course of action that neither of us knew anything about. I didn't think to ask if there were any side effects, or what were the rates of success or failure, we just took the prescription and went on our way with our instructions and phone numbers for the various clinics that would routinely scan me and take my blood.

For the first time in a while we were filled with hope and excitement, we were finally on that ladder to parenthood, and it felt that somehow we were being productive, which therefore gave us the illusion of control.

How naïve we were. Not even the most pioneering of doctors could really have control of something as unpredictable and as complex as procreation. Mother Nature is the only person who can ever claim to be in control of that situation. At the time my faith was strong and so I believed that if I prayed hard enough and continued to do all the things that made me a good person, then by the grace of God I would finally become pregnant.

CHAPTER 11

When I returned home that afternoon, I telephoned the doctor to make an appointment for as soon as possible; they suggested the following week and we settled on two days later. I then consulted my diary to work out when my next period was due and calculated the date of what could be conception. It was at this point that my mild obsession became a huge obsession.

Two days later at the doctor's surgery I convinced him to give me the drugs on a National Health prescription, and persuaded him that the local NHS nurse should actually administer the injections. You have to remember that fertility treatment in those days was relatively new and there were no concrete guidelines as to who was entitled to what treatment and where. The private health care companies were paying out for investigations and hormone abnormalities, and I fell under both those categories, and the National Health doctors were happy to share in the treatment and support of these patients.

So with a National Health prescription worth hundreds of pounds in hand, I left the surgery and went straight to what would soon become my local chemist. He didn't have any Pergonal or HCG so he ordered it for me and I was to return the next day to collect it.

By my calculations I would not be starting the treatment for at least a week, so there was nothing left to do now but go home and work on my state of mind. After all, a positive psych must help.

I thought of nothing else, I spoke of nothing else. I bought magazines that had articles about success stories, I watched programmes on television about pregnancy and giving birth, and I never really stopped smiling and hoping. I thought that any negativity would hinder the process so I tried with all my might to stay positive throughout.

And so it came to pass, a week later I started my period. I had to go to see Dr Gayle on the first day, and she gave me my first injection in the top of my leg, and then I had to go to the diagnostic clinic in Harley Street for my scan and blood test. It all seemed quite straight forward; there was a wait for both the scan and the blood test, but nothing too terrible, and there seemed to be a few other women waiting for the same treatment.

I think it was on the way home that my leg began to feel a little bruised, but nothing that I couldn't handle. But on arrival I opened the car door and went to swing my legs around and it felt like my left leg had completely seized up. It felt like I had done an extremely energetic aerobic class and pulled every single muscle in the top of my leg. Perhaps it was because I was not used to the strength of the drugs and I felt sure that it would only become easier with each injection. I was filled with optimism; if the drugs had this effect so quickly on my leg, then what would they be doing to my ovaries?

I found movement really quite difficult for the rest of the evening, although by the next morning I was able to raise myself off the chair without assistance. I didn't have to have an injection that day, but I did have to phone the surgery and arrange to have my injection the following day. I was not expecting this to be quite as difficult as it proved to be in the end. I asked the receptionist for an appointment with the nurse, and explained to her why it was imperative that the appointment must be made the following day before 12 noon, to which she replied that the first available appointment with the nurse was next week. Okay. I tried to remain calm as I explained to her in no uncertain terms that the next week would be too late and Dr Lightstone had agreed to the nurse giving me my injections when necessary. She then put me on hold for at least ten minutes and eventually came back to me saying could it possibly wait until the day after tomorrow. NO, I COULDN'T WAIT. It was then that it suddenly occurred to me that perhaps it was true that all doctor's receptionists were not really of the "human variety", certainly not the thinking human variety. When she realised that there was no way I was going to change my mind on this issue she reluctantly gave me an appointment for 11.45 a.m. and told me that in future I should give them more notice, to which I responded that in the future it was very likely that the same thing would happen again, at least with the first injection. However, I was hoping that in the future the only reason that I would be coming to see the nurse would be for my antenatal appointments. I then proceeded to make the appointments for the rest of the month and assured the receptionist that they were subject to change.

I went for my injection at the allotted time the next day, and my leg seized up just as it had done before. The nurse was surprisingly friendly and very sympathetic, and actually spoke to me about what I was going through, and even offered help and advice whenever I needed. I briefly reiterated to her the saga I had been through to get to see her and she assured me that it would never happen again.

When I left the surgery that day I was actually overcome with emotion. That was probably the first time since all of this baby business had begun that someone had spoken to me like I was not just an irrational spoilt woman wanting something that I couldn't have. That nurse had spoken to me as though what I was going through was real, and she understood how I was feeling inside, how the need for a baby was more than just a want, it was a physical and emotional yearning that hurt right down in the core of your being, an uncontrollable desire that can cause so much pain that the hurt is almost tangible. I remember that day feeling that perhaps I was not alone in this after all. There were people that I could turn to, and I thought to myself that I was really pleased that I would have to return to see the nurse in a few days.

The following day I went for a scan at the diagnostic centre. As I lay on the table, cold jelly squirted onto my very flat belly, Mr Mirth the radiologist spoke encouragingly as he passed the handle over the jelly looking for something that hopefully he would find without too much difficulty. He commented that there were at least six or seven follicles growing on both sides and that some looked riper than others. Looking good, he said, and I remember being filled with hope and optimism.

A follicle, by the way, is the sack that holds the egg inside the ovary. Most people release one egg a month, from either one or other ovary. Because of the drugs that were being injected into my body, my ovaries were working overtime and producing rather a few more than the usual one a month in the hope that when the last injection of HCG was given that one or two of the eggs would be ripe enough and then be fertilised. However, it also depended on the right amount of the necessary hormone being in the right place at the right time, which is why when I left the scan place with results in hand I had to then go for a blood test somewhere else in Harley Street. Those results would be sent to Dr Gayle when they were ready. My final stop was Dr Gayle. She also commented that all was going to plan, she stuck another needle into the top of my leg and sent me on my way with a promise to see me in three or four days to decide when the final injection should be given. Oh, and before I forget, she gave us some rules about having sex this month. We could have sex as many times as we wanted up to day twelve of my cycle, then we should wait until the day of the final injection, and it was a good idea to hold a freezing cold flannel under the testicles during ejaculation as this increases the activity of the sperm, and therefore increases the chances of a successful cycle!

Well, that was food for thought. Is a flannel held under the cold tap cold enough, or should it be kept in the freezer or fridge? And when do we prepare it for action, before or during foreplay, or maybe ...? The mind boggled. I decided that would surely have to be Martin's department. I had enough to worry about, what with a stiff leg, and a stomach that was swelling to three times its normal size as a result of eleven more follicles than usual, and the tenderness to go with it, sex was something that under these circumstances I wouldn't normally consider.

The next few days passed with visits to the doctor, attempts to behave normally, both in and out of the bedroom, and lots of healthy eating and drinking. Day eleven I went back for my scan. Mr Mirth greeted me and I prepared for the cold jelly and the handle. Well, it appeared as though at least three of the follicles were ripe and ready for action. Mr Mirth was most enthusiastic and I left the scan place feeling quite excited.

Dr Gayle was very happy with the scan results and suggested that we have the last injection two days later, according to her that would be the best time. We were to return to Harley Street on the given day for one more scan and a final blood test, pop in to see her and she would administer the final injection.

It is very difficult to put into words the way I felt when I stepped out onto the pavement in front of her rooms. The last week and a half had seemed almost unreal. I had gone through all the motions and now the time of reckoning was almost here. It suddenly occurred to me that the pressure was now off me and on Martin. He had to perform on schedule and not just once, for the few days after the last injection we were going to have to assume the positions of rabbits, and only leave the bedroom for food and when absolutely necessary. The blinds were going to be drawn, the flannels frozen, dirty videos stacked ready for inspiration, and magazines waiting as an insurance policy.

And so the next three days passed with an air of expectancy, excitement and also trepidation and uncertainty.

CHAPTER 12

My last injection was administered by Dr Gayle after my usual scans and blood test. As soon as the last injection was given we were to go home and do the dirty deed as many times as humanly possible. Romantic it wasn't. When dog breeders set out to impregnate their bitches they wait until the correct season, they find the perfect partner for the bitch, and then when the time is right they travel miles in order for the two parties to come together and have sex with a purpose. Well that is a little what it was like for us, it was sex with a purpose, without even the animal instinct that two mating dogs enjoy, even though their coming together was in fact totally contrived.

It must be said that I think Martin deserved a medal because he had to perform, all I had to do was lie back and make the right noises, and then when all was done, I did five minutes of bicycles in the air (that's when you lie on your back, and put your legs as far into the air above your head as possible, and then pretend that you are riding a bike in that position). My theory was that by doing that little exercise the sperm would be forced into the uterus faster and would have to fight against gravity to come out the other direction. I knew it only took one sperm to make a baby, but the more there were heading in the right direction, the more likely it would be that one might make it. It was also part of the strategy to stay lying in bed with my legs slightly raised on a couple of pillows for at least an hour after each session.

So romance did not even enter the bedroom door, in fact I don't think it even entered the front door. The next forty-eight hours were spent at home eating, having sex, watching a little television (thank goodness for my supply of videos) and sleeping rather uncomfortably with my legs slightly raised. Then came the waiting game.

Martin went to work, and I pottered, walked Miffi the dog, visited friends and neighbours and prayed. Within a few days of the HCG injection my breasts became extremely tender. That must be a good sign. I had read enough books to know that one of the first signs of pregnancy was sore breasts. Then after a few more days I started to feel a little sick every morning or at least I thought I did. I was so optimistic that I went out and brought a pregnancy test for the day that I knew my period would not come. Curiously on about day twenty-six my breasts no longer were quite so tender, although I was sure that I needed to go to the toilet more regularly. Then the next day my usual monthly three spots appeared on my forehead, but I was still sure that these could all be the first signs of being pregnant.

Day twenty-eight I woke early, ran to the toilet, and when I still hadn't started my period I ripped open the pregnancy test, and spent the next thirty minutes moving the stick at the right moment into each separate little pot for the time that was written on the packet. As I lifted it out of the final pot, my hands were shaking and I felt all dizzy. I could hear my heart pounding in my ears and chest, and that one second felt like it could have been twenty minutes, but the stick hadn't changed colour. I held it up to the light, took it out into the garden to make sure that there wasn't a tinge of blue somewhere, but it was white; according to the stick I was not pregnant. However, the packet did say that the test may be repeated in three days. That was it I thought, I had probably jumped the gun, and in my usual impatient manner had done the test too early. I was not ready to admit failure. I had to be pregnant, all the scans and blood tests showed that there was no reason for it not to be successful, and we had done everything we possibly could in the conception department. All my friends were falling pregnant after one month of trying, so I had to be pregnant, I couldn't not be.

I took the dog for a run in the park after lunch that afternoon, and when I came home I went to the toilet for the thirtieth time that day, and there to my utter horror and dismay was my period, in full force. The signs were all there in the last few days, but I had chosen to ignore them. I had convinced myself that the treatment had worked, and at that moment I hated myself. How could I have let myself believe that all was going to work out? What made me think that it could have possibly been so easy.

I was destined to struggle for a child, someone up there wanted to make my life a little harder than everyone else's, and it was at that moment that I realised that I probably wouldn't fall pregnant for a very long time. There was nothing else I could have done. It was a perfect cycle. We had done everything right and if it hadn't worked this time than why would it work next time or the time after that.

And so we went through the same thing month after month. The only things that changed were the amounts of Pergonal that were injected and the regularity of the injections, and the presents that Martin bought me after each month's disappointments. The first month he bought me a box of chocolate, the second a piece of jewellery, and various other things including a fur coat and an Escort Cabriolet that was all dressed up with ribbons.

Looking back at those times though, however hard they were, we were completely united as a couple in our goal. There was never a time when Martin said that he no longer could take it anymore, or that he needed a break from it. This was probably the one situation in the whole of our marriage, both then and now, in which I controlled the course of action that was to be taken.

One of my closest friends with whom I had grown up with in Brighton telephoned me during this time with the news that she was expecting her first child. I congratulated her and told her how wonderful and exciting it was, and that we were here if she needed anything at all. When I eventually put down the phone, I sat in my chair and cried like a baby. I felt as if someone had taken out my heart and stepped on it and broken it into a million pieces. It was the first time in my life that I had experienced jealousy and I was crying both for that and for the feeling of total helplessness that being infertile had caused.

I eventually came to terms with the impending birth of my closest friend's child, and life once again settled into a routine. Until one day my sister Stephanie decided to air her opinion about our state of childlessness. She was sat at my table one Friday night eating her chicken soup, chatting about her week, when she announced that she was quite sick of hearing about our treatment, and in her opinion we were becoming completely obsessed with it all, and that we should lighten up and forget about having a baby for a while. It should also be mentioned at this stage Stephanie was young, free and very single, and had no idea that maternal instincts even existed. Even so she had hit a nerve that was so raw that I ran into the garden closely followed by Martin, and we then proceeded to have the most dreadful argument, with him saying that perhaps Stephanie did in fact have a point and me responding like a completely deranged animal with no sense of reason what so ever. Stephanie had now grown tired of listening to us argue and helped herself to the next course, because as a mere student she only had a proper meal when she came to my house for dinner.

The argument went on for most of the evening, and Martin realised, or maybe decided that it was in his best interests to realise, that having a baby was the most important thing in the world to me, and the fact that many of our friends were either falling pregnant or giving birth, served to make this situation even more unbearable.

Stephanie on the other hand would not realise our anguish for many years, until she was ready to begin on her road to parenthood.

CHAPTER 13

We carried on this way for the best part of 1987. Every month we went for scans and blood tests followed by appointments with Dr Gayle. Different strengths of Pergonal were being injected at varying intervals.

I remember on one occasion, I had been to see Dr Gayle and she had given me an injection of about ten ampoules of Pergonal, which was probably the highest dose possible at one time. My leg started aching before I had even left her rooms. I stepped out onto Harley Street, the heavens had opened, and I needed to find a taxi to take me back home to Borehamwood. I limped to the edge of the road and after ten minutes managed to hail down a taxi, but when he heard where I needed to go he refused my fare. After two more drivers had refused to take me home I eventually decided to take a taxi to Martin's office in Knightsbridge. Remember, I had no way of contacting him in those days, mobile phones were not common, and the ordinary housewife such as me was certainly not worthy enough to own one. I was almost unable to walk, and I was very wet, and very cold, and extremely fed up with this way of life. I sat in the back of the taxi feeling extremely angry; angry with the drivers that wouldn't take me home, angry with the stupid injections that almost made me immobile for the best part of ten days out of every month and furious that it seemed that there really was no point to any of it because I still was not pregnant, and then my flood gates opened. I started to cry, quite controlled to begin with just quiet little sobs, but by the time I reached Martin's office and had walked up the stairs to reach his room, I was sobbing, great big huge gulping sobs, and with each sob it felt like there was so much more left inside that I couldn't stop. I didn't go in to see him for at least twenty minutes by which time I was a little more composed. I walked into his office and announced that I couldn't do this anymore and that I thought that it was time that we looked into adoption.

Adoption. That must be a simpler solution; no pain, no more injections, no more sitting in the bath pounding my breasts knowing that they had stopped hurting because the treatment had not worked, no more presents to try and make me feel better, no more Harley Street. The time had come to look into the adoption possibility.

We carried on with the treatment, but at the same time we started to research the best way to adopt. We went to meetings run by the council, and support groups that were solely for people who wished to adopt and who had already adopted. At the time there were many babies being adopted from Chile and South America, and we decided that Paraguay would be our best option. We had been given a list of all the documentation needed, and telephone numbers of solicitors that we would need to contact that were in Paraguay. It was these people that would hopefully find us our baby and co-ordinate the adoption from over there.

We contacted the various social workers and psychologists that would give us the necessary references, and we also needed Police reports declaring us honest citizens, and birth and marriage certificates that would prove that we were who we said that we were.

Whilst all of this was going on I was becoming more impatient. Suddenly there was a possible solution, and although I desperately wanted to be pregnant, and go through all the childbirth and buy maternity clothes, and be sick in the mornings, I realised that even without doing those things I could still maybe have my baby that I longed for with every bone in my body. At the end of the day I wanted a baby that was mine, I wanted a child to call me mummy, and I wanted to wake in the mornings to the sound of a baby's chuckle. Now I felt that I would have my wish, one way or the other, and I didn't want to wait any longer.

So at the end of 1987 I told Dr Gayle that I felt that the course of action we were currently on was not working and she agreed that it was probably time to review the situation and try something else. However, we agreed to give it one more month of injections and then have a break for a month and if I still wasn't pregnant then I would have a laparoscopy to double check that there were no blockages or adhesions left from the ovarian cyst that I had had the previous year.

By the Christmas of 1987 it seemed that things were finally under control. We had a plan with the fertility treatment, and if that hadn't worked after a few months we were off to Paraguay. For the first time in a very long time I felt a little more optimistic that there was a light at the end of my tunnel, and I knew that by the end of 1988 I would be a mummy one way or the other.

CHAPTER 14

I decided to write a diary in 1988, which was somewhat ironic as this was the year that would change our lives forever. Perhaps I knew that this was going to be the case when I began writing, but I always look back and think, why that year? What made me document that year and not any other?

I woke on New Year's Day at the Portland Hospital, having undergone a laparoscopy, which showed that everything was clear, they couldn't find anything wrong with me, and I actually felt that although I should be happy I really wasn't. I was home by mid morning, feeling tearful, confused and incomplete. The end of last year ended on a high, but after the results of the laparoscopy I felt as though I really couldn't take any more. Martin always assumed that I was like a Superwoman copy, strong and indestructible. But I felt the complete opposite, completely deflated and vulnerable, and wishing that if only I could see into the future then at least I could prepare myself for any eventuality.

People say words of comfort in times like these that in reality are often the opposite, and the most common words of comfort for us at that time were, "Don't worry, you are still young". I wished that they would say nothing at all, because those words made me so angry. Everyone that came to see me that New Year's Day reeled that little phrase off their tongues before they had even said hello.

When my friend Michelle came to see me that afternoon, Martin was really rude and snappy, he was finding her pregnancy harder to deal with than I was, and that made me feel even worse, because I had to work even harder to ensure that Michelle didn't notice how revolting Martin was being.

My mum always said that the best remedy for these situations was a good dinner. So she made our first meal in 1988, which was as usual really lovely, and then my two sisters, my parents and any remaining guests left and we went to bed.

I decided that it was time to distract myself with another interest, so I took a part time job in a nursery, and joined an amateur dramatic company. Life became a little more settled for a while. I resumed my injections and tried to work with a limp. I really enjoyed the rehearsals. No one knew me, I was not Daniella who couldn't have a baby, nor was I Martin's wife. I was whoever I wanted to be, and although it took a while to gain confidence, once I did, I really began to enjoy myself. Sunday afternoons for me were total escapism, and I loved them.

The morning of 29th January, Michelle phoned before I left for work to announce the arrival of her son Adam. Of course I was absolutely delighted for her, and when she said that she would understand if I didn't want to come to the hospital to see the baby, I cried for both her compassion, and also because she had the most precious gift in the world and I couldn't even do what I was created for, and that is to reproduce. Isn't it so that Mother Nature created the female of any species in order that procreation could take place and therefore the line could be continued? I was unable to perform the sole function that Mother Nature had intended. I was a dud, a half female, the runt of the species. However, Michelle was my closest friend, and it wasn't her fault that I couldn't reproduce, and I did have to go to town to have an injection and scan that afternoon, so I would be right around the corner. No matter how selfless Michelle was in not expecting me to go to the hospital to see the most precious thing in her life, I would have to be even more selfless and put her before my feelings and myself.

And so after my scan and my injection I took a cab from the bottom of Harley Street to the Portland Hospital to see the latest arrival. Baby Adam really helped me out that day. He was a bit like a baby monkey. Even his grandma said that she didn't think he was a very attractive newborn. For me it was a blessing, because when I held him I did not feel at all broody (I think I must stress at this point that as Adam grew he became more and more attractive and he is now an extremely good-looking adolescent). It must be said that one of Michelle's greatest gifts to me was the fact that her first born was extremely ugly on that first day of his life.

I left the hospital and took a cab home, and after I had slept off the effects of the injections and the emotional rollercoaster that I had been on that afternoon, we went to some friends' for dinner and drank ourselves into blissful oblivion.

Baby Adam was circumcised eight days after his birth in keeping with the Jewish custom. We both were not selfless enough to attend the service, although I went to see Michelle later in the day. Seeing her breast-feeding her tiny little bundle, so dependent and so helpless, stirred all sorts of emotions and feelings: maternal, jealousy, joy for her, sadness for me, love for **Adam**. So many to cope with all at once, so even after only an hour I felt totally drained.

I left their house that day, and went into my very small and comfortably cosy home and began to prepare our dinner. On turning on the waste disposal, water and chewed up food started seeping through the bottom of the kitchen cupboard all over the kitchen floor. It was the straw that broke the camel's back. I began to cry and scream and stamp my feet. I felt frustrated, angry and heartbroken, I felt as though I was being wound up like a toy and the spring was so tight that very soon I would be spinning uncontrollably around my tiny little house, and no one would ever be able to stop me. I had to get out. I left the water and chewed up food and took Miffi and went for a very long walk until I had calmed down enough to go home and sort out the mess on the floor, and the mess in my head.

CHAPTER 15

I felt better the following day and continued with my monthly routine. I went to Harley Street for a blood test, and the blood test place had moved to a new posh place up the road, so that made for a little variety. There were no injections today. If I was pregnant I would know in the next few days. I already knew that I wasn't, because my breasts had stopped hurting, and that was a really bad sign. I remember thinking as I stood prodding them in the bathroom mirror, that it would be nice if I was proved wrong, just for once, and every month I would push the negative feelings aside in the hope that perhaps this time they were reacting how they should if I was pregnant.

Two nights after I had badly bruised my breasts, I had strange dreams. I dreamed that I had given birth to beautiful twins, and then I dreamed that my breasts were no longer hurting because they were in fact filled with milk, and they had started leaking milk all over my bed sheets. Then I woke up to discover that all they were, were dreams, because whilst I was having those wonderful dreams of motherhood my body had other ideas, and I had started my period. Yet another month of failure, all my hopes and dreams shattered once again. I couldn't imagine coming to the end of a month to discover that the treatment had worked. I was sick of being told that it was a perfect cycle, and how wonderful my reaction was to the drugs that were being pumped into my bloodstream. If it was so perfect, and my reaction was so wonderful why the hell was I still not pregnant?

Both Martin and I decided that we would give the treatment one more month and then we would try GIFT (Gamete Intra-Fallopian Transfer), a new fertility treatment where the eggs are mixed with the sperm and then injected into the Fallopian tubes. The aim of GIFT is to allow fertilisation to occur in the right place and implantation at the right time.

I resumed the treatment that week. Dr Gayle told me that she really didn't know why the treatment had not worked that month. Everything had looked so promising. Once again this was all that was needed to open the floodgates, and I ended up sobbing uncontrollably in her consulting suite. That visit was concluded with a rather large dose of Pergonal being injected into my behind and I left her rooms deflated and limping.

I stepped onto the pavement outside her rooms recalling that very first cycle. How optimistic and filled with excitement we had been, how we were just counting down the days until we became parents, and now we had given ourselves just one more month until we were to pursue another avenue. Our optimism was no longer there; we seemed to be going through the motions so that we could say that we had tried everything. Although we both wanted the end result more than anything in the world we had lost our innocence along the way. We had grown up, and the sparkle that we once had seemed to have been left behind.

At the next appointment with Dr Gayle she told me that the reason the treatment had not worked the previous month was because the drug controlling the lining of the womb was not the correct dose. I felt that she was giving us an excuse in order to be given the chance of another month of treatment. Another chance to pump different doses of different hormones directly into my system, another month for me to limp around like a disabled person, another month of my stomach becoming distended to three times its normal size, and another month of waiting for my breasts to stop hurting so that I could feel that awful dread and know that once again we had failed. We gave her that last month.

As if to reinforce our resolve that it was time for a change of tactics, when waiting for an injection at the doctor's surgery, I was sitting next to a lady who was also waiting for an injection. She told me that she had been trying for a baby for fourteen years, and had had three failed attempts at GIFT. I promised myself that day that there was no way that I would give up my life to injections, scans and blood tests, only to be met with disappointment month after month. I would have adopted twelve years ago if I had been her.

A few days after that injection I decided to hand in my notice at the nursery school. I was no longer finding it therapeutic working with such young children. In fact it was having the reverse effect. I was becoming increasingly depressed. All my emotions were at the wrong levels. The drugs were making a difficult situation even more difficult. I was extremely sensitive, and totally uncontrollable. Working with children was not the ideal situation, and it was time to bail out.

D-Day (the day that we had to have sex like rabbits after the final injection) arrived and went with a rush of sexual activity. It was actually D-Three Days! And thankfully two of those days this month were a weekend. Halfway through the weekend there seemed to be an unusual amount of coming and going of my neighbours outside my house, and then at about mid morning Martin came and dragged me away from my bed. He told me to follow the ribbon that was attached to the front door. I followed the ribbon out to the side of the house and toward the garages where all the neighbours (who were also our good friends) were waiting and chatting. The ribbon led to our garage; inside which was a beautiful metallic blue Escort Cabriolet. I had always wanted a convertible car, and Martin knew that I loved the Escort. It was a wonderful present, but I knew as he did that it was supposed to be a diversion, or as I had come to know them infertility presents. What could possibly follow a car!

This month was slightly different from all the previous months, because this month I had an injection after D-Day. This apparently was to maintain the lining of the womb in order for the egg to implant itself. I can honestly say that we really were not expecting it to make any difference at all, and we were right.

As usual my period started on time and without delay. I felt the usual pang of complete devastation, but this time I pulled myself together, and phoned the Portland Hospital. They had recently opened a Fertility Unit, and I made an appointment with one of their doctors to discuss the possibility of GIFT. I also resolved to start getting all the necessary papers ready to put into motion the adoption process, as soon as possible.

CHAPTER 16

March 1988 was probably one of the most significant months so far. It was the first month that I was not going to be on any treatment at all for nearly two years. I left my job at the nursery, which was a huge relief. We also decided that it was time to look at moving into a larger house.

We went to the Portland Hospital to meet someone about starting GIFT and were terribly disappointed. The doctor that we met was almost like a salesman that had been employed to put you off the idea. We had a 25 per cent chance of it working at all and it was going to cost about £2000 a try. We both came away feeling really depressed. GIFT was expensive and therefore we could only afford one attempt, and then if it failed we would have to take out a loan in order to go to South America to adopt a baby.

The day that we went to the Portland we went to a talk about adopting a baby in this country, and that made us even more depressed. Although we did have our age on our side, we were Jewish, and parents that put their babies up for adoption had the right to choose which religion the adoptive families should be. The majority of parents chose their own faith, and there were very few Jewish babies that were put up for adoption. A British Jewish baby was unlikely to be an option.

Martin during this time seemed to take on a different personality. He became extremely demanding and controlling, and would often come home and start an argument with me about trivial things, like the fact that I hadn't tidied the house properly, or that I hadn't taken his shirts to the cleaners, and I spent many nights crying myself to sleep, feeling guilty that

I had let him down, and that not only was I unable to provide him with a child, but I really was not a very good wife either. My self-esteem at this time was at rock bottom, and it felt very lonely and quite scary.

It seemed also that whilst Martin was working very hard, he managed to find time to play golf and snooker, but when I asked for time to talk about our plans or maybe for him to come home and have a meal with me or to get involved with preparing our papers to adopt, he was much too busy, and very short tempered. So I spent my days cleaning, cooking, on the phone to psychologists, and meeting with social workers and doctors, in an attempt to have all our papers ready to go and get our baby should the GIFT fail, which was very likely. I also had to run all the errands that Martin had given me before he left for work to ensure that he would have nothing to be angry with me about when he returned home.

One night Martin came home and announced that he didn't want to do the GIFT. He wanted to go straight to South America. I still don't know to this day why he felt that way, but I suspect it was something to do with the cost and the fact that the likelihood of it working was so slim, he may as well be throwing £2000 down the toilet. But I had to try everything to have a baby of my own before I went to the final option. So I managed to convince him that we had to try just once, and then I promised I would never ask anything of him again.

Stephanie and my friend Michelle were my rocks at this time. Mum and dad were fantastic, but they were not around the corner, and mum was so emotional about my pain that I found that I did not want to make it even harder for her. Stephanie had absolutely no idea what I was going through, but her innocence and total detachment of the situation was my support. She would listen to me moan with half an ear, and then we would spend the rest of the afternoon eating chocolate and cheese and onion crisps whilst watching a video. She at the time was in the process of getting a career on the stage; consequently she had a lot of free time on her hands.

Michelle was around the corner, and her home was always open. Even if I just wanted to pop in and have a cuddle with Adam, she was fine. I could also tell her how desperate I felt, and she understood my maternal instincts, unlike Stephanie, who didn't have any. They were the core of my support system, and then there were my neighbours, Jacqui, Jill and Tracy. They lived in the same close, and we all spent a lot of time in each other's houses.

They all knew that when it was D-Day our house was out of bounds for at least forty-eight hours, and they also knew when to bring the bottle of wine round at the end of each failed attempt. It was because of all of them that I didn't become a manic depressive. When I cried they helped me through and made me laugh, when I wanted to talk they would listen, and when I wanted to party and drink myself into oblivion they usually joined me.

My parents were there as my mum and dad. A girl always needs her parents, even if it is just for a cuddle and a reassuring squeeze. We went to Brighton to discuss all our options with both sets of parents. Both sets said that they would support us in all our decisions, but my mum has since admitted that she thought that we were too young to have been considering adoption, and that she felt a little uneasy with the idea of IVF but she was happy with the GIFT. At the time all we wanted to know was if we adopted a baby would they be able to love it as much as one of our siblings' natural children. They all said that it would not even be a consideration and that of course there would be no difference at all.

At the end of March I went back to the Portland Hospital to see the consultant regarding starting the GIFT. We decided that I would start injections the next week on the first day of my period, and then the procedure would be carried out approximately two weeks after the first injection. We put a provisional starting date in the diary, because I would need a scan on day one or two of my cycle, then I would need to start injections immediately. Mr Smith was a really lovely man with a perfect bedside manner, and I was much happier when I left than I was the time before.

I stopped off in Holborn on the way home that day to pick up our copy birth certificates to send off to South America. Then that evening Martin and I went off to Oxford to see a psychologist in order for him to assess whether or not we were mentally stable enough to become parents. I thought that it was quite bizarre at the time, because how many children were born into abusive families or families that really didn't want them, with the main missing component being love, and here we were passionately pursuing a dream of becoming parents, putting ourselves through every possible scrutiny, and these people still needed proof that we were the right "sort" of people to become parents. If every pregnant mother had to pass the same sort of tests as we did in order for them to keep their own child, how many of them would actually experience motherhood?

However, we were told that evening that there wouldn't be a problem and that he would recommend that we be considered for becoming adoptive parents. When we eventually returned home that evening I felt that I was on a high. I felt positive and alive, and the light at the end of the tunnel was coming closer, and I could almost touch it.

CHAPTER 17

I t was coming up to the Jewish festival of Passover, which lasts for eight days. This festival actually involves a lot of work. It is to remember the coming out of slavery of the Jewish people from Egypt, and to commemorate this we have to eat different foods. The people when they left Egypt didn't have time to let their bread rise, and so we only eat foods that have no raising agents in for those eight days. It has also become a tradition to do a major spring clean around the time of the Passover to ensure that there are no crumbs or crusts of bread anywhere in the house, not even on the ceiling! Being a good God-fearing Jewess I spent the next few days cleaning harder than ever. Martin really had nothing to moan about, his house was truly spotless and crumbless. I did break for a couple of hours to go to the doctor to collect my prescription of Pergonal, where they informed me that this was the last month that they would be able to give me a prescription for these drugs as they did not want to be liable for any long-term side effects. Well, I have to say I felt a little tremor of concern at these implications. Was it possible that twenty years down the line they might find that the drugs I was pumping so freely into my body may become responsible for some dreadful disease? I put my concerns into the very back of my mind and resolved to make sure that I would do my very best never to think about them again.

The next break from cleaning was to go with Martin to view a house, and lo and behold we both really liked it and put in an offer immediately, which was accepted. Now all we had to do was sell our house.

I eventually finished the cleaning of our house and it was so clean you could have eaten off the floor. It was time to go to Brighton to be in the folds of my mum and dad's home, where at least I knew that for a few days I would be looked after, and I really needed that at this moment in time. We collected Stephanie en route and eventually arrived in Brighton at 1 a.m. By the time we had had a cup of tea and unpacked the car, I collapsed into bed at 2 a.m.

Jacqui, my neighbour, phoned me early the next morning to tell me that she had given birth to a little girl called Emma, a sister for Daniel. I didn't cry, I just imagined how it would feel to be making those calls, informing my nearest and dearest of such wonderful news. I wasn't sure if I would ever be in that position.

I spent the next couple of days visiting friends that I hadn't seen for a while and basking in the warmth and security of my parents' home. My period, however, was late. I was supposed to be starting my treatment on 5th April and I still had not come on. I knew that I could not possibly be pregnant, the thought was pushed immediately to the back of my mind, although at certain intervals during the day it had a tendency to push its way forward and my heart would give a skip of anticipation, maybe after all this I was pregnant. I had heard of stories about couples who had tried everything and almost given up and then by some miracle had fallen pregnant all by themselves. Maybe that had happened. When I spoke to the Portland the next day to postpone my appointment, they told me to phone them when I did start my period, or I was to do a pregnancy test in a week if nothing had happened. To hear those words "pregnancy test" made my hopes real. I really believed that it had happened when we least expected it to. Mum and Martin knew what was going on, but neither dared to voice any optimism.

All my hopes were shattered on the 6th when I started my period. Matters were not helped when my good friend Andrea phoned to say that she had just given birth to a little boy Elliot. I tried really hard to be strong, I knew that I couldn't be pregnant, those sorts of miracles don't happen to me, but my heart felt like it was broken, and my chest felt like it was being pulled apart; I was completely devastated.

Martin of course was extremely upset, but he chose to show this by being really horrible to me, totally unsympathetic and very self-centred.

He was no comfort, and I had to get away from him that evening so I went to see a friend and I took a bottle of wine with me. I soon felt better.

I phoned the Portland on 7th April and they decided that I needed to be scanned the following day. I had intended staying in Brighton for the weekend, but that was not to be. I packed my clothes, food parcels from mum and my mother-in-law, dog basket and dog, put the roof down on the car and headed back home. It was a tearful goodbye. I felt like I was on the last leg of a journey. It was our last attempt at becoming pregnant. If it didn't work we would have to become parents another way. In three days I would be twenty-five; what would this year hold for me? Would I be a mummy by the time I was twenty-six?

The next day was our wedding anniversary; we had been married four years. They had not been easy. As we opened our cards sitting up in our bed, Miffi curled up at the end, I felt that we were being tested. Our relationship so far had undergone stresses that very few other people of our age had had to deal with, and when they had they often resulted in a split. I did not want to be another statistic. We had to get through this together. I wanted to be opening our Tenth Anniversary cards together with not just a dog sitting on the end of the bed, but also at least three children, although ideally I had always wanted six.

After lunch on the day of our anniversary we had to go to the Portland for our first scan. It seemed to take forever. I really have no idea what they were looking for. I do know that there was no one to talk to after the scan and we were sent all round the hospital looking for a doctor. We eventually found a secretary and had to make do with her. Her main concern at the time seemed to be our method of payment, and when we left we both felt extremely discouraged and totally pissed off.

Two days later it was my birthday and there was snow on the ground. I don't ever remember snow in April. It was supposed to be spring, but no, the winter had returned. My parents joined us from Brighton and in the evening of my twenty-fifth birthday we went with Tracy and her husband Lee to a pub in St Albans and sat by an open fire drinking champagne and dreaming about our futures. Would champagne ever be drunk to celebrate a new arrival and would the arrival be in the human form? Or perhaps we would just have to get another puppy and make do with that. Now there was a thought!

CHAPTER 18

Typically British, the weather for the next few days was proper spring weather. The snow was like a final goodbye from the winter. I tried to keep my routine as normal as possible. I had my injections at the doctor's on days five to seven, and then on day eight I had to go to the Portland for a scan and an injection. We were kept waiting for ages, and Martin ended up losing his temper with the doctor. He began ranting that he felt that the hospital was more concerned with our cheque books than with us and that they should be more compassionate and realise that we were going through the biggest trauma of our lives. I just wanted to hide under the table, and I wished that Martin had left his temper at home, but it came everywhere we did.

Eventually, I had the scan. It was the most humiliating thing I had ever been through. Martin decided to wait outside. The radiologist was extremely discreet, and covered me from the waste down with a blanket, but I didn't even know that vaginal scans existed let alone that I was going to have one. Apparently, they are more accurate than normal scans, and they needed to know how many follicles there were, and exactly what sizes they were.

After my ordeal, Dr Connor took us into his room and very patiently and kindly took us through the procedure and explained what to expect next. This happened to be a needle in the bum for me. I felt terribly uncomfortable that Martin had been so hard on the team. I knew that in a private hospital they had to make money, but the doctors and nurses all seemed very kind, and I did feel that they were interested in my feelings and well being. I felt like I was in the best place when I left that day; I was happy that the team at the Portland were looking after me, and Martin would have to learn to like them too.

Day nine, I went to the Portland for a blood test, took the train home and later in the afternoon went to the doctor for another injection of Pergonal. I was beginning to feel like a pincushion. My legs were very stiff, and now my arms were beginning to look like a heroin addict's might.

Stephanie came with me on day ten, and this time the probe of the scanner was absolutely massive. It was the most dreadful experience. I tried to take my mind to another place, and when that didn't work I tried counting the ceiling tiles, and when that didn't work I tried to look at the scan screen, but nothing worked so I just willed the experience to be over, and hoped that I wouldn't have to go through this too many more times. I then had another injection and was sent on my way.

Martin came with me into the scan room the next day, and when the scan was over he had a slightly greener tinge to his complexion. Mr Smith informed us that my follicles were now fully formed and that I didn't need any more Pergonal, but I was to return tonight for my final injection.

There were all sorts of emotions to deal with that morning. Martin and I had shared an intimacy during that scan. He had witnessed some of the indignities that women had to suffer, and seemed to have a new respect, and I also found a new respect for him. I thought that he would not be able to cope with seeing a vaginal scan, and he handled it with maturity and integrity. He did not make one joke or innuendo ever and just filed the experience into the deepest corners of his memory.

The afternoon seemed very long that day. My parents came and had lunch with us, after which the boys played golf. My dad had to go up North on business, so Martin and I drove my mum to Victoria Station. We then came all the way home to sit in front of the television for a couple of hours. Then at 11 p.m. we drove two cars into town. We left Martin's at the garage for a service the next day, and then we went to the Portland for the final injection.

It was strange being there in the middle of the night. The corridor lights were dimmed and there was an eerie silence to the ward. An occasional buzzer pierced the stillness and behind the reception desk doctors and nurses talked in hushed conversation. One of the night staff met us and took me into an empty treatment room where at precisely midnight, and not before, she gave me the injection. We left the Portland Hospital at 12.20 a.m. and went home where I had to endure a fitful night of strange and disjointed senseless dreams.

Tuesday 19th April 1988 I woke at 6 a.m. I hurriedly cleaned the house then had a bath and hair wash, followed by a brisk walk around the block with the dog. We arrived at the Portland Hospital at 7.45 a.m. I was shown up to my room and Martin was taken down to the department where he would have to produce his sperm. He was armed with his *Playboy*, whilst I chose easy reading and brought with me a *Woman's Own* magazine. Considering the task at "hand", Martin was back with me relatively quickly. I didn't really enquire as to his well being, I assumed that his contribution had gone to plan. I was taken to theatre at 9.10 and after a little prick in the back of my hand was out like a light.

I woke an hour and a half later feeling very sore, very sick and very shivery. I couldn't focus on anything and I felt like my mouth wouldn't close. They wheeled me to my room and Martin and mum were both there waiting for me. The first thing I said was, "No more I've had enough". At which point both mum and Martin started to cry, and because I didn't want to feel like the odd one out I cried with them.

Mr Smith came to see me a little later in the day to tell me that they had managed to take out seven eggs in total. Some were better than others, so they had put four grade "A" eggs back and were going to fertilise three in test tubes to make sure that Martin's sperm and my eggs were in fact compatible. This was actually very significant, because if the eggs in the test tubes were unable to fertilise with Martin's sperm, then it was unlikely that the eggs that they had put back into my Fallopian tubes along with the best of Martin's sperm would be able to fertilise. We would have a result from the test tube eggs before we would know what was happening to the eggs inside me.

I was home in my bed by 6 p.m. and that is exactly where I intended to stay for at least a week. I was going to give myself the best chance possible. In spite of the advice to carry on as normal, I didn't feel normal anymore. I knew this was our last chance of having our own baby, and I was not going to do anything that may jeopardise our chances. The safest place for me and my eggs were in bed, and so that is where the waiting game began. I was doing everything in my power to feel like I had some kind of control, and whatever happened next was in the hands of God. I hoped that just this once he was looking down on me, and felt that I deserved the chance of becoming a mummy.

CHAPTER 19

I spent the first week after the GIFT doing practically nothing. I stayed in bed all morning, and then would come downstairs in the afternoon to sit either on the couch or in the garden with my feet up. I did no cooking, cleaning or washing. Stephanie and Michelle came in to see me during the day to walk the dog or make me my lunch and to ensure that I didn't move very far, and then the neighbourhood watch team, Tracy, Jacqui and Jill, made my dinner in the evening, and sat with me for the twilight shift before Martin came in from work.

My only outing was to the doctor to have my stitches out, and that was in Stephanie's Mini; not a very smooth ride at all. By the end of the first week I must say that I was extremely bored. The second week I did start pottering, doing the washing and some very light housework, plus I had to start cooking again. I felt that I was becoming a meals on wheels recipient. I hated to be dependent on other people, and I had to keep reminding myself that I was doing this for a very good reason and that I wasn't really helpless, but I had made the decision to do as little activity as humanly possible in order to give the eggs inside me the best possible chance, and it was a decision that I was not going to reverse. By the end of the second week I began to think about the possibility of all my actions being in vain. Although I did not want to imagine the possibility of success, it was terrifying to imagine failure.

My nights were filled with irrational dreams, broken up with endless trips to the toilet to make sure that I hadn't come on, and then in between the two, my mind would real from all the endless possibilities. What if the

GIFT had worked, what would happen then? What if it hadn't, then what? And how would we cope? My days were filled with television and mindless activities and then at night my brain would wake up and cause havoc.

Sometime during the first week, the hospital had telephoned us to say that two out of the three eggs in the test tubes had indeed fertilised, which was extremely good news for us as it ruled out incompatibility. We also had to decide if we wanted to freeze the fertilised eggs. We decided that we didn't want to and so the hospital threw them away. We did not allow ourselves to think about the implications of those actions.

We had been told that any time after day twenty-two there was a possibility that I may come on if the treatment had not been a success. So from then on I became a nervous wreck. I went to the toilet every half an hour day and night; I became distracted and unfocused and was unable to concentrate on anything. I tried to read my book and ended up reading the same lines over and over again. Time seemed to stand still and I wished that we could bypass the week that we were in and be in the following week where I would know one way or the other, and then I would no longer have to speculate and prepare myself for any eventuality.

On day twenty-five my younger sister Joanne came to see me, and when she saw me she commented on how tired I was looking and that it was a little odd as I had done nothing at all that might exert myself. I pushed the thought into the back of my mind because when thinking logically I came to the conclusion that stress on its own is exhausting. I was experiencing broken nights and extreme anxiety. My heart would sometimes feel that it was beating so fast that it might burst out of my chest and into my mouth. All of this and nothing else could explain the fatigue that I was feeling. The following day after breakfast I felt extremely sick and ended up throwing up in the downstairs toilet. Once again I pushed the implications to the back of my mind and again blamed the experience on nerves.

At 10 a.m. on day twenty-seven, I phoned the Portland and they told me to buy a pregnancy test to do first thing in the morning. I was terrified, I knew that it was going to come out negative, but I had to do it just to make sure. I had the feeling that I was somehow delaying my period, because I didn't want to come on. It was still only morning time and an awful lot could happen in one day. It was going to be a very long afternoon.

The day didn't turn out as expected. I went to sleep in the afternoon for an hour, and when I woke up, I had started to bleed. Devastation hit, I called Martin and he drove straight home. We both sat crying for a long time. It felt like it was the worst day of my life, the despair and emptiness was just beyond belief, and I felt so wretched. How was it possible to go through everything that we had already endured, seemingly doing everything we possibly could in order to give the process the best chance and it not work? What else was there left to do? I had done everything right and still it seemed that was not enough. At that moment right then I felt that whatever we had done we were destined to fail. We phoned our respective parents to tell them the awful news, and mum told me to have a nice hot bubble bath and a very large brandy. I had the bath but really didn't fancy a brandy. The pain would still be there when I became sober again.

At 2.30 a.m. on Wednesday 4th May 1988, I went to the toilet and lo and behold the bleeding had stopped. I went back to bed and tried to go back to sleep but to no avail, once again the thoughts ran through my mind. Why had I stopped bleeding? Would it all start again in the morning? This had never happened before. What was the plan? Should I do the test or not? I had it there burning a hole in the drawer next to my bed. Every half an hour I checked to see if the situation had changed, until finally at 5.30 a.m. I knew it was time. I went to the toilet armed with my Clear Blue Predictor test. In those days it took half an hour to get a result. You had to put the stick into three different pots for ten minutes each and after the last pot, if the stick had turned blue then you were pregnant; white meant that you were not and I knew only too well how it felt when the result was white.

It was the longest half an hour of my life. I sat downstairs reading my Stephen King book (or should I say pretending to read), and every ten minutes I returned to the bathroom to take the stick out of one pot and put it into the next. As I took the stick out of the last pot, I could feel my heart beating in my chest, my ears were pounding, and beads of sweat were forming on my forehead, my hands shook as I drew the stick that could change my life out of the last hole. IT WAS BLUE, IT WAS POSITIVE! I ran screaming into Martin who was up until then still asleep and oblivious to the night's events. I held the stick under his nose and shook it screaming, "I'm pregnant, it's positive," over and over again, tears streaming down my face in total disbelief. It took Martin at least a minute to register what was

71

going on, and being the eternal pessimist his reaction was not quite what I expected. He started questioning the accuracy of the test. He made me lie with my legs raised in bed for the rest of the day just in case it all fell out! When we told our parents they were overjoyed and quite shocked as only the day before they were getting used to the idea that we would soon be off to another country to adopt a baby. They had to change their emotions from grief to elation in only a few hours, and they also had to search for the correct things to say to us, because I am sure they must have thought that if things could change one way so quickly then surely they could just as easily change back again. I certainly was not aware at the time of how it must have been for all of them, but on reflection I can appreciate that their journey was also a rollercoaster of emotions and that it probably was neither easy nor natural for them to cope with all that was expected from them. We decided not to tell anyone else until the pregnancy was confirmed by the hospital and we were a little further down the line.

The next day was yet another hurdle. I woke at 6 a.m. and did a sample in a bottle, not one of the easiest things that I have ever done. I managed to get the majority of the urine down my arm, but there was enough in the bottle, and that was all that mattered. We left the house at 9 after Martin had walked Miffi, and we had had breakfast. My first outing in over two weeks was to the Portland Hospital for them to analyse my wee. It was twenty times worse than any exam I had ever taken. All sorts of thoughts were going through my mind. What if I had done the test wrong? What if the test was out of date or a dud? Maybe it was all a huge mistake.

After half an hour Dr Conway walked into the room and confirmed that the test was positive. I was pregnant. We were going to have our baby. Everything had been worth it, and I didn't have to do it again. I was fixed to my seat, I couldn't move. It was all so overwhelming. Martin just stood grinning like a Cheshire cat, patting the doctor repeatedly on the back saying "thank you" over and over again. After the shock had subsided a little we sat and chatted. We asked the usual questions, is there anything we should or shouldn't be doing? And we also asked about the chances of having twins. Dr Conway told us that there was only a 25 per cent chance of twins and increasingly less of a chance for anything more. We had gone to him for one baby and that is all we wanted. Now I just wanted a normal healthy pregnancy. I could go home and start looking at maternity clothes. I could join in with the conversations about babies and teething and breastfeeding. I could discuss my increasing breast sizes, and be just like all my friends who were either pregnant or just parents. I had never felt so excited about anything, and as we drove home I put my hands across my stomach and stroking it gently I was filled with pride; I was carrying our first child. It was truly a miracle and I was eternally grateful.

CHAPTER 20

I knew all about the symptoms of pregnancy, morning sickness, tiredness, and fuller breasts, but I did not expect them to materialise quite as quickly as they did. I dared not complain because this is what I had been dreaming of for the last four years, and being of an extremely superstitious nature I thought that complaining would tempt bad luck. However, I was hit with all the symptoms with incredible force. I was sick at least three times a day and often in the night, and the tiredness was like nothing that I had ever experienced before. I could not get through the day without at least a two hour sleep during the afternoon. I never woke up before ten in the morning and I was usually asleep by ten at night. If we had evening arrangements I would have to sleep in the late afternoon otherwise I would not be able to stay awake past the starters and would find myself falling asleep in my chair. And when I slept if I rolled over onto by stomach the pain from my breasts was so intense that it woke me, and if anyone should accidentally bump into me tears would come to my eyes. They were like tender rocks and were completely off limits to Martin. Having said that my body was completely off limits, I told him that he knew how to use his hands, as was apparent because I was pregnant and his hands played a rather large part in the process, so now he would have to carry on using them if he felt that he needed some relief in that area. Because my hormones were also playing up and were causing extreme mood swings Martin dared not argue with me, so I assumed that he was happy with the arrangement.

Our life was relatively normal in the two weeks following my positive test. I did not do any strenuous activity although I still took the dog out for walks. We went to friends' and they came to us and we entertained family. We decided to tell only a handful of people i.e. family and Lee and Tracy. No one else knew, and no one suspected. Because I thought that the GIFT had not worked I had told all the people that were important on that day that I was not pregnant, and if I hadn't Martin had, so no one thought anything different. My clothes, however, were beginning to feel a little tight, which I thought was normal, but looking back, given the amount that I was being sick I should not have been noticing any expansion in my waist size.

When I was six weeks pregnant I woke one morning went to the toilet and noticed that I was spotting. I was gripped by this terrible dread. I knew that things had been going too well, nothing could be smooth for us. I wasn't really sure of the implications of spotting, but I tried to reassure myself that I would not have so many symptoms if there really was something wrong. After referring to my rather large pile of pregnancy books that were growing on my bedside table we decided to phone the Portland and they suggested that we go and have a scan. It is very hard to describe the emotions that we went through on that morning driving to the hospital with our own thoughts. I didn't want to believe that anything was wrong, but I didn't want to be optimistic because I had to prepare myself for the worst scenario. My heart seemed to be beating too fast, and the seatbelt seemed to be getting tighter, and I couldn't remember the hospital being so far, and there certainly had never been so much traffic. Time seemed to go at a snail's pace that morning and the journey took forever. We arrived at the scan room and I went to change my clothes into a gown and a fluffy white dressing gown; although it was eighty degrees outside I was shivering. We were seen quickly and shown into the scan room where there was a radiographer and Dr Conway. The cold jelly was squirted onto my tummy and the probe run across. Both the radiographer and the doctor were looking intently at the screen and both were pointing. Then Dr Conway pointed more deliberately. "There's one," he said and then he continued, "and there's another one, and another one and another one". He repeated himself again, this time showing us a screen and pointing out four sacks that resembled my follicles in the early stages of my treatment.

I couldn't really grasp what he was saying and Martin didn't speak at all. I asked the doctor to explain, at which point he then told us that I was carrying quads. How could that possibly happen when we were told that the chances of that happening were 10 per cent of nothing? Now what were we supposed to do.

I dressed and went into another room where it was explained that it was possible that one or two of the sacks may be empty and that may be the reason that I was spotting. We then obviously wanted to know what would happen if none of the sacks were empty and I was in fact carrying four babies. What were the chances of them surviving, and how difficult would the pregnancy be? Everything had suddenly changed; this was not going to be a lovely straight forward pregnancy. I was told that there was no reason to worry at the moment, there were lots of sets of quads in the world, and although I would probably have to spend the majority of my pregnancy in hospital, with careful monitoring and lots of rest, the babies stood a very good chance of survival. We were told that we must be very aware that the chances are that one or two of the sacks will probably not develop and quads at that moment was unlikely to be the end result.

We couldn't really speak very much on the way home. I had so many mixed emotions. All I had wanted was to be like every other pregnant woman, and now that was definitely not going to be the case. I didn't know if I wanted any of the sacks to be empty, but on the other hand did I want four babies all at the same time? I was confused, excited, happy and sad all together. This was so enormous neither of us really knew how to deal with it, there is nothing that can prepare you for a situation such as the one we had found ourselves in. It was almost too much for one brain to cope with. It was so abnormal that I didn't know how to react. I couldn't find the relevant emotions and I almost became numb and detached. There really was nothing we could do; I didn't feel that I needed to cry nor laugh and I wasn't angry or particularly worried. This was just so alien, there was nothing that we could refer to in the past to help us know what to do and so we did the only thing possible and decided to take one day at a time.

CHAPTER 21

The next couple of days seemed as though we were in a fairy tale. Things like this didn't happen to real people. I spent hours wondering if there could possibly be a happy ending to this story.

I had become famous overnight. We had decided to tell everyone that I was pregnant, and with quads. The reactions that we received were a great source of amusement. My house had suddenly become like a bus station, people in and out with offers of help, and loads of cakes! So there was not really a chance for the impact of our news to sink in.

Two days later the spotting became bleeding, and it was suggested that I spend some time in hospital where I could be monitored more closely. So I packed a small bag, made arrangements for the dog, made all the appropriate phone calls and left for the hospital, where on arrival I was put into a wheelchair and taken to my room. Here I was told to undress and get into bed where I had to stay. I was only allowed out of bed to go to the toilet. Mr Smith arrived and suggested another scan so I started drinking. An hour later I was wheeled down to the radiography department where the scan showed that all four eggs were still intact although one was slightly smaller than the others. It was thought that this might be the possible problem.

I settled in to hospital routine very quickly, my phone was always busy and there were constant visitors. I actually didn't have any time to get bored, in fact I was grateful when there was a quiet time because I was still feeling very tired and sick and now to make things even more difficult I had started having nose bleeds. I looked like shit and felt even worse and was trying to hold on to any thread of normality that there was, and my visitors provided those threads.

I had been admitted into hospital on Friday 20th May 1988 and on the Wednesday evening I started bleeding again quite heavily. I was confined to bed again and a scan was arranged for the next day.

So the following day, with bladder full, once again I was wheeled down for yet another scan. This time we could see the heartbeats and everyone in the room was marvelling at them when a fifth sack carrying a fifth embryo with a fifth heartbeat appeared on the screen. I remember laughing and thinking that it was all becoming a bit ridiculous and then I remember feeling quite frightened. I had to have an internal scan at the same time to make sure that there were actually no more than five. Thank goodness five was the final bid.

It was a bit of a mystery where the fifth embryo had come from. Only four eggs had been put back during the GIFT. It was possible that one of the eggs had split and I was carrying one set of identical twins and it was also possible that when piercing the follicles to extract the eggs one was released but not removed. Either way it was too early to tell and not really important because the fact was that two weeks ago I thought that I was expecting a baby and now I was expecting five.

We spent the rest of the day thinking and discussing the implications of having five babies. Firstly, how many were likely to survive, if any? And then if they all made it, how difficult would it be to raise them? Our lives would never be the same again. Martin was extremely worried about this and felt that we should consider selective reduction. This meant that two or three of the babies would be killed.

I felt very differently. I knew that life with five babies would be very hard but I knew that I would cope. I didn't want to kill any of my babies. I thought that the fifth baby was a miracle, it was put there for a reason and I had already messed with nature enough, and by reducing I also ran the risk of losing all of my babies. There was no question in my mind by the end of that day. I was going to give all my babies my best shot. I would do whatever it took to get them to a stage that they would be able to survive outside the womb. I told Martin, however, that I would go and see the professor at Queen Charlotte's and that I wouldn't make a decision until I had. I still had a few weeks **to** worry about that. Now I had to try and put all my energies into keeping my babies alive.

The next few days were extremely emotional. Martin and I argued and just couldn't seem to see things the same way. His main concern was that our marriage would not survive the ordeal of raising quintuplets, and my main concern was would I be able to keep them inside me until they were strong enough to survive.

Mr Smith did not seem too happy about the fact that I wanted to keep them all. He really believed that the pregnancy would not be a success. I agreed to listen to all the advice that was on offer and not make my decision until then. But in my head the decision was made. And as I spent more and more hours of each day being sick, I knew that there was no way anyone could persuade me to go down any other route.

Within a couple of days Mr Smith and Martin and my parents realised that my resolve to carry these babies as long as possible could not be broken. I did find it quite daunting when Mr Smith tried to explain the size that I would get to by the end of the pregnancy. He told me that my stomach would never be the same again and even with surgery it could never be corrected. He said that if I reached twenty-eight weeks I would probably come out with one baby, twenty-nine weeks with two, and each week after that one more.

The nurses took me up to the sixth floor to see the Special Care Baby Unit. In the unit was a baby born at twenty-six weeks, and although he was tiny he was so perfectly formed and only needed a little oxygen to help him breathe. This strengthened my resolve further. I knew that my babies would be born early, now I had to work really hard on looking after myself and them to ensure that they stayed inside long enough to give each one a good chance of survival.

During the next few weeks I spent a lot of time being sick, a reasonable amount of time sleeping, I had constant nose bleeds and I cried loads. The nurses had become my friends and I couldn't really remember what the outside world looked like any more. I had become institutionalised and the thought of going home was really scary.

On Friday 10th June, nine weeks pregnant with five babies in my tummy, I went home. It was a really hot summer's day and the smell of the car fumes mixed with the heat made me feel really quite nauseous. I went home to a spotlessly clean house and lots of food parcels from all our neighbours and friends. It was lovely to be home, but the journey had exhausted me, so I slept for a couple of hours.

When I awoke the next morning, the sun shining through the yellow blinds shedding a warm glow over our bedroom, I forgot momentarily the task that lay ahead, and when I awoke fully the realisation hit me and I was filled with a feeling of excitement, trepidation, fear and worry. What would the next few months have in store for us? Would we ever be able to look back at this time and laugh or would it fill us with a terrible sense of loss? I stroked my stomach gently and felt proud that I was given the chance to carry these babies that would grow together inside me, and I knew that from this day they would be my focus. Nothing else would be as important, I wanted to see the day that I would hold each one in my arms and kiss them gently on their cheeks and sing quietly in their ears as I lay them down to sleep in their cots.

From that moment I became theirs. Nothing nor no one would be able to understand how it was to be totally consumed by the need to protect and nurture the babies that were now totally reliant on my actions. I was completely responsible for their survival, and I had to find a mind set to cope with this. I became almost self absorbed, but not in a selfish way; it was the only way I felt that I was able to protect them. I could not allow weakness or doubt, I had to be strong and resolved and I really believed that if I gave myself to them I would be able to shield them from any dangers that may come their way. From the moment that I saw the fifth tiny heartbeat I knew that I would never again be the same; deep in my soul I had changed.

CHAPTER 22

The afternoon of 14th June was a hot and balmy one; one that made sure all the smells and fumes from the road and cars stayed around long enough to make my morning, afternoon and evening sickness significantly worse. Mum (who had stayed with us for the last couple of days) and I took a taxi to Queen Charlotte's Hospital to see a professor regarding selective reduction. In spite of sitting in the front of the cab with all the windows open we still had to pull in quickly at a service station so that I could be sick. I did try to explain to the taxi driver that I was carrying quins and that I was feeling sick most of the day, but he couldn't grasp the fact that it was possible to carry more than two babies and kept talking about my twins. I didn't even try to put him straight. Talking induced vomit!

When we arrived we were shown into another scan room where I was instructed yet again to change into a gown, and then they scanned me. I saw all my babies' hearts beating, and we could even see the umbilical cords. It was the most amazing sight and I knew that very few people in this world would ever experience being able to see five of their children's hearts beating together inside their womb, feeding off them through a little thread. Every movement, and every beat of their little hearts was because of me. How many women can say that they have been able to do the same or experience that same feeling? It really was quite humbling, to know that my needs were now secondary to theirs, and that I was almost a human incubator. I also felt honoured that I had been chosen to encounter this.

Thankfully all the decisions were taken out of our hands, because when speaking to the professor he explained to us that selective reduction had recently become a criminal offence. I don't know what would have happened if we had been adamant that we wanted to reduce, because I know that there were plenty of reductions performed after that date and are probably being performed right now. I am sure that there must have been ways around the legalities, but thankfully I didn't want to know them and so the decision was taken away from me and I could now concentrate on nurturing the growing bundles inside of me.

The summer passed fairly smoothly. I settled into a routine of throwing up, eating, sleeping, cooking, going for short walks with the dog, and more sleeping. My house seemed to be constantly busy and my phone never stopped. However, when I was tired I left whoever was sitting downstairs and went to bed.

I had a check up with Mr Smith when I was ten weeks pregnant, and although he said that I could do more than I was probably doing, I decided that I didn't want to take any chances. I later found out that he thought that my quintuplet pregnancy was a bit of a disaster and that maybe if I carried on as normal that I would have an early miscarriage.

I spent a weekend at the end of June in Brighton and saw all my friends from when I had lived there. And all the time my stomach was getting larger and larger. By the time I was twelve weeks pregnant I looked like I was five months pregnant. Nothing fitted me anymore, and I was wearing my friend Tracy's old huge all in one jump suits that she had kept from another era. She used to wear them with a belt, I couldn't!

The exhaustion was really the greatest problem, and I was becoming forgetful. One night I put on a saucepan of water to boil for some pasta, and an hour and a half later I smelled burning. When returning to the kitchen I found my saucepan very black, very steaming, and extremely smelly. On another night Miffi needed to go out at about 1.30 a.m. so I let her out and went back to bed and waited for her to scratch at the door. Three hours later I heard her howling outside, I felt terribly guilty as I ran downstairs to let her in.

My emotions were becoming increasingly irrational as I became larger. I felt terribly insecure and worried that Martin no longer loved me, and I questioned his fidelity. I knew that my fears were unfounded, but however rational I was in my thoughts, my heart had other ideas. Thankfully we were able to discuss my worries and Martin did everything to reassure me that there was absolutely nothing to worry about.

On 21st July I was fifteen weeks pregnant, but I looked like I was at least thirty-two weeks pregnant. I went into town for another scan. I felt really nervous, I didn't know what to expect; so far every scan had brought different surprises. Once again I changed into my gown and fluffy white dressing gown and lay on the bed.

The scan took an hour and a half and it was the most emotional and surreal experience that I had experienced up till that day. The babies were all kicking and waving and jumping around. We could see all their arms and legs, and their little hands. Each baby had to be measured and checked, and they were all the correct size for fifteen weeks, which was fantastic news because usually in a multiple birth all or some of the babies are smaller. They all had long legs, which no one seemed concerned about so I just thought that perhaps we would have tall children. The results of the scan filled everyone with more optimism, even Mr Smith seemed encouraged, and so we went home feeling happy.

July passed and I grew larger and slower and extremely hungry. I could eat any man under the table during those weeks. My energy levels were very low, and I looked as though I was ready to give birth. However, Mr Smith was very happy with the way things were progressing.

On 4th August Martin went to Portugal for a few days, and I went to Brighton. Martin leaving me left me feeling vulnerable and alone. I was really frightened to be without him, and even when at my parents' home I needed him there. I phoned him and he phoned me at least ten times a day, and in the end he cut his trip short and came home.

The weather was beautiful in Brighton, in fact it was so hot that my dad had to blow up the rubber dinghy and fill it with water so that I could sit in it to cool down. I have to say I resembled a very large whale in my maternity costume. My belly button had popped out and was sticking through all my clothes, and when I lay flat the babies would start kicking and my stomach would move in all sorts of different directions. It was very unusual that they were all asleep at the same time, one of them if not all of them would be moving constantly, and very often there was a foot or a hand in my bladder which meant that my trips to the toilet were becoming more and more frequent. However, when I rested my hand on my tummy and one of the babies would kick in response I felt the most overwhelming love and emotion. I wanted to protect these little souls from all harm and I wanted to keep them in the safe and warm forever, because I felt that there inside of me I was in control; I could control their destiny and I didn't want any thing to change that.

On 11th August I was eighteen weeks pregnant and having a lovely holiday with my parents at their home in Brighton. I woke in the morning. Martin had gone to work in London and had left whilst I was still sleeping. I went to the toilet and noticed that things were not quite the same. I was not really worried, but I phoned the hospital to be on the safe side. They advised me to come in straight away to make sure that everything was still as it should be.

After a scan that showed all babies alive and well I was told to go home and take it really easy, and to stay in bed as much as possible. I felt scared and worried. All of a sudden my nice snug little world was coming to a halt. I had been so optimistic and now I didn't know how I felt or what I really wanted. It would have been so easy to let it all go and give up and then just get back to normal. Martin and I loved each other, but this was all such a strain. All we had ever wanted was to be a happy normal family. I didn't mind a few stresses and strains because I felt that they made you appreciate the good things more, but sometimes I felt that someone up there had a vendetta against us. I had known that the pregnancy was going to be hard, but it seemed that I always followed the hardest road, and I was getting tired.

And so I went home to bed.

CHAPTER 23

I spent the next couple of days in bed, again just getting up to go to the toilet. The bleeding gradually subsided and after a few days I was able to go and sit downstairs. A few days more and I went for short walks, but I was not permitted to hold the dog's lead in case it pulled in the wrong direction.

I settled quickly into a routine of "first" breakfast at 7.30 in the morning then back to sleep for a few hours. Then "second" breakfast anytime between 10.30 and 11.30 a.m. after I had washed and dressed, and I usually went downstairs to eat that one. This was followed by a short walk, which became shorter and shorter as the days went on because I was becoming larger and larger. Lunch was usually at about 1.30 p.m. after which I went back to sleep for at least two and half hours. When I awoke I would have tea, and then play some scrabble or watch some television, after which I would have some supper. Someone had to help me in and out the bath as I was now so large I was worried that I may slip or even worse, that I may get wedged in the bath and not be able to get out. I sometimes had my bath in the morning, it really depended on who was around and when. If I bathed after supper I would then have to eat something before I went to bed and then by eleven o' clock I would go to sleep.

On Thursday 25th August I was twenty weeks pregnant and I went into town to see Mr Smith for a check up. I went with my mum and Martin met us there. Well, it was a very thorough check. He checked the size of my waist, which was forty inches, and the height of the womb, which was thirty-three inches, my blood pressure was fine and my cervix was closed. All my babies were alive and kicking (and boy were they kicking).

The next six weeks were critical, I had to be very careful and take it really easy. It was therefore decided that on 5th September I would be admitted back into hospital where I would stay until it was time to have the babies.

Although we were entering the final stages of this pregnancy I had to convince myself that we still had an awfully long way to go, and actually we did have a really long way to go. The next few weeks were going to be the hardest, and I knew that I was not going to breeze through them so easily, but I had to take each day at a time, and it is very difficult to imagine how something is going to be if you haven't experienced it before. So whilst I was aware that the last few weeks were not going to be as straight forward as the ones just gone, my ignorance was bliss and I approached the task ahead with the same calmness and fortitude that had already helped me to this point. The future of my babies depended on me keeping them inside me for as long as possible and I was the only person that could make that happen. I felt that I had sole responsibility. The doctors could only monitor and give their advice, Martin could hold my hand and bring me food and flowers, but the responsibility lay with me. If I gave up now my babies would die. The enormity of the task at hand was terrifying, except I couldn't take it all on board at the time, and it is only when recalling the events that I am able to acknowledge the weight of the responsibility. Although I am sure I did feel some strange emotions at the time, I think I subconsciously decided it was safer not to analyse those feelings. And so I just focused on doing the best thing possible, and that was to stay calm, have lots of rest, and listen and take heed of every bit of advice given.

Things were becoming strained all round. On Saturday 27th August, mum had made lunch and Stephanie was round. It was a kind of farewell lunch, as the next family get together around anyone's table would be after I had given birth, so emotions were running deep. Martin at the time didn't smoke on a Saturday as it was the Sabbath, and that made his behaviour very volatile and irrational. Well, just before lunch we were all sitting in the garden when out of the blue he called Stephanie a "wanker" and she promptly hit him around the head at which I burst out crying and ran (or should I say waddled) upstairs with Martin and Stephanie hot on my heels. They then proceeded to argue, with Martin hurling a string of abuse in Stephanie's direction, at which point she burst out crying and locked herself in the toilet. Mum ran upstairs and also started crying, at which point Stephanie came out of the toilet and announced that she was leaving and ran out the front door with Martin following. Dad then decided to get in on the act and started packing to go home to Brighton. He was also not smoking for the same reasons so his mood left a lot to be desired. Poor mum was running between everyone trying to be the peacemaker, and worried sick that all the emotional activity would set my blood pressure soaring and not be very good for the babies. She somehow managed to calm everyone down and we eventually all sat down to lunch, and realised that the strain was beginning to take its toll.

The next few days passed uneventfully. I carried on with my usual routine the only difference being that I was becoming increasingly lethargic and my appetite was decreasing. I was only able to manage small meals, and so mum fed me little and often.

My last weekend was terribly emotional. All my friends popped in to see us, and my sisters were both lodging in the back room. I felt like I was going on a trip to the other side of the world and when I eventually returned it would be as a very different person. My parents took Miffi back to Brighton with them on the Sunday night, and their leaving was terribly emotional; it took me ages to stop crying. Lee and Tracy came to see me later in the evening and once again I cried, and then when Martin packed all my clothes, night wear and toiletries, followed by books and puzzles and cassettes and cassette recorder, I cried again. I remember thinking that the next time I would go to bed in that room after that last night I would no longer be pregnant, and no one could know when that would be, and what would be the final outcome. Martin tried to hold me for a long time that night and I eventually fell asleep nestled against his arm. Who could have known what would happen between then and the next time I would fall asleep in his arms.

At 3 a.m. I had the most dreadful nose bleed and Martin spent the best part of an hour scrubbing the bedroom carpet trying to get the blood stains out. The rest of the night was spent dozing and at 6.30 a.m. we decided that it was probably best to start getting ready to leave. Everything was fairly normal, Martin brought up my breakfast and I had to sew some buttons on his shirt. Then we dressed and made the bed as usual. After which I went round the house saying goodbye to the bathroom, goodbye to the bedroom and goodbye to the spare rooms, and as I walked down the stairs I said goodbye to them too. I thought it was an attempt to make a sad situation a little better with a little humour, but Martin was standing at the bottom of the stairs sobbing and when I saw him I put my arms around his neck and sobbed with him. All I had wanted was to be normal and yet we had had to fight so hard for absolutely everything. We had to fight to be together ten years earlier, then we had to fight for the right to marry and now we were fighting to become parents. How much more fight did we have left?

At 10.30 a.m. we arrived at the Portland hospital.

CHAPTER 24

On Tuesday 6th September, after a rather fitful night's sleep, I was taken downstairs for another scan, which showed all my babies were the right size for twenty-one weeks. This was absolutely wonderful news, because the doctors really thought that by that stage of a multiple pregnancy the babies would be much smaller than they should for the amount of gestational weeks. I had lunch after my scan, but was not able to eat very much at all, there just wasn't enough room for food and babies!

After lunch I had to have another scan to see if my cervix was still closed and if not how open it was. The radiographers refused to comment, which was not a good sign, because if there were nothing to worry about they always tell you at the time of the scan. I was filled with dread. It was too early for my cervix to be open at all, it meant that labour was imminent, and it was much too soon for that.

Mr Smith came to see me within ten minutes and had to do another internal (not one of my favourite experiences), after which he assured me that everything was fine, and that my cervix was in fact completely closed. The relief that I felt was indescribable, and I knew that I could refocus on carrying these babies for at least a few more weeks.

Once again I had to find a routine. I was woken in the mornings at 6.30 so that I could have my blood pressure taken, and then I would have my breakfast about an hour later. I usually went back to sleep until about 10.30 when a nurse would come to make my bed and help me to have a bath. Some days I was too tired for a bath so I just had a wash. I then would go and sit out on the sofa in the corridor by the lift, where I would have a sandwich and watch the world go by for half an hour. It is quite amazing what one can hear and experience by just sitting and listening. I really learnt that art in those few weeks. After my half hour of world watching I would go back to my room to watch some TV or listen to music until lunch, which I didn't really eat. Lunch was usually followed by a string of visitors who I would have to try and be polite to, even though all I really wanted at the time was lots of space and as little conversation as possible. Soon after the last visitor had vacated my space I would have a sleep until supper time when Martin would come back, along with Mr Smith, and then the evenings were usually spent with an assortment of more well-wishers, and on the occasions that I didn't have any visitors I would play scrabble or cards with Martin.

On the Wednesday after I was readmitted into hospital, Mr Smith came to see me and told me that if I went into labour at or after twenty-four weeks they would try to save the babies, if it was earlier they would not be viable. He also said that up to twenty-six weeks I would have to deliver naturally, but anytime after they would deliver by caesarean section. He really didn't sound very optimistic and this made me very anxious; all I could think of was that we might come out with nothing. To go through all that we had, to come out with nothing was unimaginable, and didn't bear thinking about. I had been so positive before I had come into hospital, but as each day passed, a little more doubt was put into my mind. I couldn't bear to lose any of my babies; they were all doing so well growing together inside me, and I felt that each child that didn't survive would leave a space in my heart that no one would ever be able to fill. During the first few days whenever Mr Smith came to see me I felt he was more and more pessimistic, and my moods mirrored his.

Sunday 11th September was the eve of the Jewish New Year. Steph, mum and dad came to see me and they had brought me a dress that looked like a tent, and a pair of slippers that I couldn't put my feet into, because they were now so huge and swollen and resembled two very plumped up cushions on the end of two very large legs. They stayed a while and left in a rather emotional state as this was the first time that my family had not been together on the New Year. As it was a very spiritual festival anyway it felt like our heart strings were being tugged very hard.

Martin stayed the night at the hospital, and we lit the candles and ate apple and honey (which symbolises a sweet new year) and then we played some scrabble, cried down the phone to mum and dad, then both went to sleep.

I was now on all sorts of medication. I was taking calcium pills that dissolved in water, Build Up milkshake because I couldn't really eat very much, pills to help me sleep, pills to stop contractions, iron pills because I was becoming increasingly anaemic and pills to stop me itching. I had developed a hormone itch and often had to go and sit in a bicarbonate of soda bath in the middle of the night to try and relieve the irritation. I had to wear white tight socks to stop thrombosis, I continued to have really bad nosebleeds, and my gums used to bleed all the time as well; all in all I was not a pretty sight. In fact I avoided mirrors at all costs; it was too scary to see what I had become.

On Saturday 17th September I had my usual string of visitors during the day, and the amazing thing was that some of them I hadn't seen for years. I am sure that I was becoming a bit like a museum piece, people probably thought that they would never have the opportunity to see a lady carrying five babies again so they had to take the opportunity by the hand. In hindsight I should have probably charged a nominal price per viewing. I was still at the stage, however, that I was quite polite and made small talk with anyone that wanted to. I was feeling, however, very tired by the time everyone had left that evening and fell asleep watching a film at about 11.30 p.m.

At 2.30 a.m. I woke in terrible pain; it was so piercing that I couldn't actually move my arm to reach the buzzer to call the nurse. It seemed to engulf my whole body and I felt like someone had knocked the wind out of me. I didn't know what to do and began to panic, but the pain subsided, so I moved the buzzer closer and went back to sleep. Twenty minutes later the pain returned, but this time I could reach the buzzer and a nurse came rushing in and gently stroked my tummy and held my hand until the pain had once again subsided. I was having contractions and Mr Smith was called immediately. He gave me a double dose of the pill that stops contractions and said that now we would have to wait and see what happens. The pains never returned and I went back to sleep feeling shaken but not stirred!

My visitors were limited after that, and things settled down again for a while. I had two outings that week. One was up to the seventh floor where the rooms have balconies, so I was able to sit outside and breathe some fresh air for the first time in a couple of weeks, and then on another occasion two of the nurses took me in a wheelchair to Regent's Park where we had an ice cream, and they had a walk and I had a ride. I felt like a little girl being wheeled around in a buggy, and so excited to see normal people doing normal things. I wonder now what they thought when they saw me being wheeled around looking like someone had blown me up with a bicycle pump, no shoes on my feet, eating an ice cream like I had never eaten one before. I wonder if I would have looked twice at someone like me on that day, but I was smug in the knowledge that I was carrying my five precious babies and I felt that I was more special than anyone else in that park. I was so proud to be in that wheelchair in that park because I knew that I had been given a unique gift.

On Tuesday 20th September I had another scan. My cervix was stretching a little more than last time, but not worryingly so, and they measured all the babies, except number two who wouldn't stay still long enough to be measured. They were all doing so well and were such good sizes that I couldn't help being encouraged. In two more days they would be viable. That was such a huge milestone.

Things were beginning to get a little tougher. I was finding it very hard to get comfortable, I seemed to be so tired all the time, I really couldn't eat very much and I was having a nose bleed two or three times a day. I was terribly itchy and the pills that they gave me for that made me even more tired and irritable, but my sleep was always disturbed because I had to wake up to change position, and my positions were limited because of my size. People were still coming to see me in a steady stream and I was getting sick of small talk, and everything seemed to be such an effort. Martin and I were very on edge. It was such a nail biting time now, every day was another huge hurdle, but we needed to be so much further down the track for the race to be a success.

On Wednesday 5th October I was moved from the Gynaecology Ward to the Maternity Ward on the third floor. It was like moving house. I felt that I was leaving all my friends behind and that I would have to make a whole new crowd. I was really frightened and felt really insecure. The nurses on the first floor knew me; they knew my needs, what made me laugh and what made me anxious. They came and sat on my bed to watch *Neighbours*, and would have tea with me in the afternoon. I had to leave that safe haven and start all over again somewhere else, it was all so traumatic, and I felt very vulnerable.

My new room was right at the end of the corridor and was slightly different from the one downstairs. I didn't like it as much and I felt a bit homesick, not for my home, but ironically for the room that I had just left. I tried to be brave, and had to make a very conscious effort not to panic. This was the room that I was to stay in until it was time for my precious babies to be born. How strange is the human nature that we accept things because we have no choice, even if we are not pleased with the situation; if there is no alternative we have to continue. We can either give in to our misgivings and fears or we can turn them to our advantage, and I would let nothing get in the way of my determination to succeed. So whilst this move was traumatic, I resolved to continue in the most positive way that I could and told myself that tomorrow would be another day and it was just a matter of time before this room would be akin to home resembling the one I had just left.

CHAPTER 25

On Thursday 6ᵗʰ October I had reached the magical twenty-six weeks, but I didn't feel any different. I had expected to feel relief or something, but I felt that it wasn't time to give up and I pushed the significance of the twenty-sixth week to the back of my mind and reminded myself that I had a long way to go. Every hour now mattered, each baby stood a 3 per cent better chance of survival with each passing day, and I prayed every minute of every hour that my babies would be healthy and happy. I felt a little guilty that I wanted them all to survive. I thought that perhaps some people may say that I was being greedy, but I had become attached to each one. Each one was my child; I had felt each kick and turn and the hiccups that would rock my body for so many minutes every day (I was sure that each baby would have the hiccups at least once a day). Guilt was something no mother should feel because they wanted the survival of their child.

It was a little odd not being downstairs and it took me a couple of days to get my bearings and find a new routine. I met another lady on the floor who was also still pregnant; she was carrying twins and was in hospital until she was ready to give birth which was apparently imminent. We were the only two pregnant ladies on the floor, so we spent some time in each other's room, having our lunches together and chatting and sometimes just watching our favourite programmes and not even bothering to talk. I also went into the nursery occasionally and chatted with the nursery nurses that were on duty. I was really slowing down though. I was not out of bed for more than an hour each day. Even sitting in a chair was not very comfortable and my legs had become so swollen that Mr Smith was happier if my feet were up, so bed was the best option.

One afternoon, Martin, mum and dad were sitting in my room having tea and I needed to go to the toilet, so Martin helped me to lift myself out of bed and I slowly waddled into the bathroom, pulled down my size twenty-two knickers and plonked myself down on the toilet, and on doing so I heard a cracking sound. When I had eventually heaved myself off the toilet I looked at the seat and it had cracked under the weight of my enormous backside; I was completely mortified. I had gone from being a slender size eight to a huge gargantuan whale that was unable to control the force of her weight. Housekeeping changed it very quickly, but the story kept lots of people amused for quite some time.

On the evening of Monday 10th October, Mr Smith arrived with an anaesthetist and a heart specialist. My blood pressure was high I had protein in my urine and fluid retention. Things were not looking so great any more, and it sort of explained why I was feeling so lousy. I was having trouble sitting myself up in bed, and even reaching across to my bedside table was a really huge effort. Martin suggested that they give me a monkey bar over my bed to help me move, and sure enough an hour later one was brought up and it really did help; I could now sit myself up without assistance.

The director of the hospital came to see me to discuss the possibility of press coverage. A quintuplet birth may arouse some interest from the press and did we want that kind of attention. We decided that after the publicity that was given to the birth and deaths of the septuplets we would rather not have any publicity at this stage. So we concluded that in order to avoid any leaks of information we would change our names, and so we became Martina and Alexander Daniels and our babies would all be the Daniels' babies. We then had to tell all our close friends and relatives that if they wanted to call or see me that they would have to use our new alias.

On Wednesday 12th October I was becoming more and more uncomfortable; my bottom felt as though it was about to give way, I couldn't breathe properly and I was always breathless, I itched everywhere, my hair needed cutting, my eyebrows plucking, my top lip bleaching, and I couldn't even see my legs and feet so I couldn't imagine the state that they were in let alone my bikini line, assuming I still had one! I had missed a whole season, all my visitors were coming to see me in winter clothes; when I was admitted it was still summer. I wondered how much longer I could carry on and also how much longer they would let me carry on. I was not able to eat very much anymore and the nurses were taking my blood pressure at least every hour, which in hindsight was not a very good sign. At the time I don't remember thinking that I was really, really ill, but my mum said that by that stage she could no longer think about the babies, she was not even sure that I would survive. I was really very unwell, but ignorance was bliss and I had no idea. I just thought that everything that I was feeling and going through was to be expected and that all my doctors had seen it all before and that they knew exactly what they were doing.

Connie the other pregnant lady was induced on Wednesday 12th October and gave birth to a boy and a girl, Daniel and Sophie, and my last walk as a pregnant lady carrying quins was to her room the next day to wish her congratulations. I was now twenty-seven weeks pregnant, and feeling very proud of myself.

At two o' clock in the afternoon on 13th October Mr Smith came to see me to tell me that the team that had been looking after me had just had a meeting and they had decided that I was going to have the babies by caesarean section on Sunday morning at eight o' clock. They felt that by that time I would have had pre-eclampsia for nine days and if left any longer it would be dangerous for me. He sat with me for a while to sketch over some of the details, but I didn't really hear much of what he said. I felt relieved, yet disappointed. I didn't know if I had held on long enough and I felt as though I had almost given up. Once I knew that the babies were viable maybe I didn't try so hard, perhaps I had lost some of my focus, but on the other hand I was feeling really awful now, and I didn't honestly know how much more I could take. Still, it was out of my hands now, the decision had been made and now all I could do was pray that my babies would be strong enough to survive the ordeal of coming into the world thirteen weeks too early.

The next few days went by in a haze. I had a scan (that was brought into my room because I was not allowed out of bed anymore unless I needed the toilet), and I remember seeing a little girl and assumed that I was having more girls than boys, although my mother-in-law predicted all boys. Some paediatricians came to see both Martin and me to discuss how they were going to help our babies and what we should expect to see when we first saw them. Nurses and doctors were in and out of my room taking my blood pressure, listening to my heart and doing lots of checks in preparation for the big day. There was an air of excitement, and everyone was extremely optimistic, the babies were fantastic sizes and I had gone a long way into the pregnancy. How many hospitals could boast the birth of a quintuplet pregnancy? I was getting more attention than the Duchess of York (she had had her baby in this hospital just a few months earlier).

Martin and I spent time writing lists of names; we had five girls' names and only three boys' names. I was convinced that I was going to have more girls than boys, after all I had grown up with two sisters and therefore couldn't imagine having a house full of boys.

On Saturday 15th October everyone had left the hospital by nine in the evening as they wanted to be back bright and early the next day. Martin went to pick up a video camera from Neville and buy a film for our still camera, and I couldn't sleep. The nurse was in and out and we chatted through the night and I watched three videos and dozed on and off in between. I was excited and scared and although what was going to happen to me had been explained in minute detail I still had no idea what to expect. I put down my emotional shutters and tried to think about other things, but the truth of the matter was from tomorrow the future of my babies that I had nurtured and loved and fed and protected was no longer going to be in my hands. I was handing them over to a team of doctors and nurses whom I didn't even really know, and there would be very little that I would be able to do if they ran into difficulties. I was terrified and possessive. These were my babies and my responsibility and I was about to hand them over to strangers. It felt like I was giving them up. Suddenly it was six in the morning and Martin and the nurse came in together, and it was time for the nurse to prep me for major surgery.

CHAPTER 26

By eight in the morning on 16th October 1988 I had been prepared for my caesarean, and I felt almost submissive; this was going to happen and I would not know an awful lot about it until I was woken after it was all over. A strange calm engulfed me, and when the porter came to take me downstairs I became completely detached from the situation and left the conversation to Martin and the nurse.

I was taken down to the sub-basement and wheeled into a little room at the side of the theatre. In the theatre there were at least thirty doctors, nurses, and theatre staff waiting for my arrival. Thank goodness I was unable to see them, I didn't look too great!

The anaesthetist gave me some oxygen through a mask over my nose and then he fixed the probes that would be attached to the monitors in three different places. He put a needle in my hand and I kissed Martin goodbye and promised to see him soon, and then I was asleep.

Some time later I was being gently woken and a faceless voice was telling me that I had given birth to four boys and a girl. I remember hearing the voice, but I didn't really understand what it was saying. I thought that if I went back to sleep I would understand it a little better when I woke up.

When I next opened my eyes I was back in my room, it was darkened and there was a nurse right next to me. I tried to speak, but the words wouldn't really come out properly. I tried to move my head, but there was a tube coming out of my neck and as I moved it felt peculiar. I could hear a bleeping noise and I was very uncomfortable.

The nurse saw me wake and repeated the fact that I had given birth to four boys and a girl, and that Martin was up in the Special Baby Care Unit with them and he would come down to see me soon. She waved some photographs in front of my eyes, but they really didn't look like anything, so I decided that the best thing to do would be to go back to sleep. In my sleep, I could hear the most dreadful sort of snoring noise, it was right in my ears and it kept disturbing me, but whenever I opened my eyes to see who was making it, it stopped. I later realised that it was me.

I had no sense of time that day so it is difficult for me to relay the chain of events accurately. I wandered in and out of sleep, and all my family came in one by one to see me. The power of speech did return, but I don't think it made much sense. Martin kept coming in and reeling off all sorts of numbers but I had no idea what he was talking about, something about the numbers I remember meant that the babies were either doing well or not.

Then some paediatricians came to see us and told us that it was unlikely that all of our babies would survive, but they would do all that they could to save as many as they could. They said some other stuff, but I couldn't understand what they were saying. I didn't take their comments on board, and the memory of that conversation is not at all clear. They did say though that the next forty-eight hours were critical and if they could get the babies through that then they stood a better chance.

As the day wore on I became more and more alert, and realised by the evening that my babies were in fact quite ill. However, they were all stable and that was a really good sign. I was desperate to see them, but I was still attached to so many tubes, and I was apparently still quite ill myself. My blood pressure was still very high and the tube in my neck went directly to my heart to make sure that they could measure my blood pressure really accurately. The bleeping was still going on and apparently that was measuring other things like heart rate and temperature, I think.

By evening all the family had left and I was left alone with a nurse. I had been given a bed bath and that really helped to make me feel better. I kept dozing off and waking up and asking the time, and each time it was only two or three minutes after the time before. It was a very long night, but by the end of it I was much more alert and could take on board more information.

Some time in the early hours of the morning a nurse came in to see me. She was a sister and had just come from the SCBU. (Special Care Baby Unit). She told me that my little girl had had a bleed somewhere, she had become very pale and they suspected that she had bled into her brain, but they would not know how severe the bleed was until she had had a brain scan and they were waiting for the scanner to arrive. She was having a blood transfusion and that would help her to pink up. I had no idea the extent of what she was saying to me. I felt an unsettling worry deep inside me, and knew that however hard it had been up until now it was about to become even harder.

Twenty-four hours after I had become a mummy I still hadn't seen my babies. I couldn't wait any longer.

CHAPTER 27

My little boys all had a relatively stable night apparently, but my little girl really had caused quite a stir. It transpired that the bleed in her brain was a Grade II bleed which was not severe, but may show itself as something like dyslexia when she grew up, but it certainly would not affect her quality of life. It had been caused by a pneumothorax, which is air inside the chest wall, and it therefore needed to be drained using a chest drain. All my babies had very immature lungs and they were being kept alive by using extremely high pressures on the ventilator and lots of medicines and tubes.

At 11 a.m. Monday 17th October the tube from my neck had been removed, and I was manoeuvred into a wheelchair and taken up to the Special Care Baby Unit to see my babies for the very first time. I really had no idea what to expect, but I knew that they were all quite unwell and that they would all be attached to an assortment of tubes and machines.

As I was wheeled out of my room the corridors were lined with flowers and the smell of the orchids hit me. It turned out that all these flowers had arrived yesterday to congratulate us on our new arrivals, and apparently there were more still arriving.

I was taken up to the SCBU in the lift along with my mum, Martin, my wee wee bag and all my drips, but I didn't notice any of them. I was filled with excitement and nervousness. I couldn't believe that I was about to see the little people that I had nurtured and loved inside me for all these past weeks, that I was about to see the little hands and feet that kicked at my insides and the little chests that used to rock my body with their little hiccups.

As I came out of the lift it was explained that the three boys that had been born first were in one room and then the little girl and the last little boy were in another room. We went to see the three boys first, starting with Quinn No. One. I was wheeled over to his incubator and I couldn't really see very much. He was all stretched out and attached to so many tubes, and so very tiny. He had on a white gauze hat that was holding a ventilator tube in place and this tube was coming from his mouth. The nurse opened the porthole in the side of the incubator and I gently put my hand inside to touch him. His skin felt like paper and I felt that it might tear. I was completely numb. I went round to all my precious new little babies and felt completely overwhelmed. I couldn't comprehend that these little souls had been inside me. They all had tiny fingers and toes and the tiniest nails, but each one was perfect. However tiny they all were it was impossible to imagine how all together they could have ever been able to fit into my stomach! I suddenly felt that I had to leave the sixth floor. I needed to be back in my room where I could digest the enormity of what was happening. I didn't react the way I had expected to. I didn't cry or laugh, I didn't feel happy or sad, I just felt total disbelief. It was almost like an out of body experience. This was so abnormal, five babies being born from a human was not natural; I was like a freak and so were my babies. They didn't look like bouncy newborn babies that I had always dreamed we would have. They looked like baby rabbits before they had fur, and they were held together by paper and were so fragile they looked as though they may break. It was so much to take in, that the easiest thing to do would be to go back to my room and watch *Neighbours*.

My blood pressure was high when I finally made it back into my bed, and I was in quite a lot of pain. I didn't think that there would ever be a time when I would be normal again. I couldn't imagine not having any pain and being able to move freely. I kept seeing the babies stretched out in their incubators, and it was so hard for me to acknowledge that they had come from me. I felt completely detached from them, after all these months of willing them to live it felt as though they were not really mine at all.

After some discussion we decided that we would name them. Quinn One was Joshua, Quinn Two was Gregory, Quinn Three was Nicholas,

Quinn Four was Jodi, and Quinn Five was Benjamin. Joshua, Gregory and Nicholas were the biggest all weighing in at over one kilo, then came Jodi who was 940 grams, and Benjamin was the smallest at 710 grams.

Tuesday 18ᵗʰ October 1988. I didn't see my new babies again until the next day when I was taken to see them by the nurse and Martin. By this time I had no more tubes and I was not so high on painkillers and therefore I felt more focused. Martin wheeled me round to see each of our babies, and at the same time he was videoing them and me with Neville's camera. Today we went to see Jodi and Benjamin first. Although Jodi was keeping everyone very busy she was relatively stable, and Benjamin was plodding along quite happily with a little frown across his tiny forehead as though he were concentrating on staying alive and seemingly doing quite a good job. We had a chat with the nurses and I told them of our plans to take our children to Israel as soon as they were out of hospital. We gave Jodi a pink balloon and Benjamin a blue one and the nurses tied them to the end of their incubators. I blew each one a kiss and went to see my babies in the other room.

The atmosphere was completely different in there. Gregory was having terrible problems. He was on maximum help with the ventilator and was being given lots of drugs through his intravenous drip, but he was still struggling. I didn't really understand what was going on, but there were a lot of people around his incubator, and I was only able to spend a very short time with him. I went to see Joshua, who was also not doing as well as he could although he seemed to be more stable, and then I went to see Nicholas. He was wide-awake and moving around, and yet he apparently was also having more problems becoming stabilised. As I left I remember saying to the nurse to please look after my baby and to please help him to live and she replied through tear-brimmed eyes that she was really trying her very best.

We returned to my room downstairs and immediately phoned the rabbi. We needed him to come and bless our children, we had to try everything to help them, and maybe now medical science was not enough. The rabbi asked if he could come the next day and we told him that he needed to come as soon as possible. He was there within twenty minutes.

During those twenty minutes Dr Millett (the paediatrician overlooking the care of all the babies) came to see us. He looked very white, very tired and very solemn. Gregory was very unwell, they had tried everything and he was still deteriorating. He told us that he didn't think he was going to live. He asked us if we wanted to go and say goodbye to him. However much you think you are prepared for the worst something inside, the optimistic part of one's brain, always expects a miracle. I couldn't give up. God had given us our babies for a reason, surely it wasn't so that he could take them right back. I felt very sick. My head started spinning and I began to hear ringing in my ears. My head was swimming and then I was sick. A nurse came in and took my blood pressure and then gave me an injection that made me float.

Martin on the other hand didn't have an injection, and lost control. He began talking irrationally and his eye movements became erratic and disjointed. He kept running up to the SCBU and his mouth kept twitching and his stutter became profound. Suddenly my biggest worry was him. He was falling apart, and I couldn't help him. There was nothing anyone could do. I couldn't even be there to help my little boy fight to live, and I wasn't well enough to hold him and help him die.

The rabbi arrived and we all went up to see the babies. I couldn't go in with him whilst he blessed them, I just sat outside in the doorway watching and quietly sobbing. My nose started bleeding and my head became light, and however much I tried to be strong my body was too weak, and I was taken back downstairs to bed.

I didn't get to say goodbye to Gregory before he died. At 6 p.m. on 18th October 1988 my second born son gave up and died. He was brought down to us wrapped in a blue blanket, free from tubes, his perfect tiny little face sleeping peacefully. His black hair curled tightly to his forehead. His little wrists were bruised from the drips and needles, but he was at peace now. No one was going to prick or prod him any more. He was an angel in heaven watching over his brothers and sister. As I held him a part of my heart died with him and I knew this moment and the picture of my baby's face would live with me forever. I held him for a long time, but he never seemed to get cold. It felt like I was holding a sleeping child, and that very soon he would wake for a feed, but he never would. He would never kick and move around as he had so happily just a few days ago, and he would never have those hiccups, and I would never see him take his first step or say his first words, and I would never have to soothe him through his first tooth. I had lost a son and it went against the order of life. A child is supposed to bury its parents when they grow old and grey, not the other way around.

They took him from me that evening and I never saw Gregory again, I didn't even have a proper picture to remember him by, and our memories of him were so few. We just didn't have enough time. I blamed myself; I hadn't given him enough time to grow. It was my fault that he was too weak, and I would carry that guilt forever.

CHAPTER 28

I wouldn't let Martin go home that night. I somehow felt comforted by his presence and thought that if he were there then maybe things wouldn't get any worse. The nurses made up a camp bed for him in my room, and we attempted to eat a meal together, trying hard to behave as though nothing bad was really happening. I felt as though we needed to behave normally, and by doing that the pain and confusion of emotions would lessen, and for a while it did.

I phoned the special care unit hourly, and the nurses looking after our babies were wonderful and patient, feeding us all the relevant information even if it was only to repeat the same thing hour after hour. Repetition at this stage was good; it meant that things were stable, at least for a while.

The nurses looking after me were concerned that I had not opened my bowels since the birth and kept giving me different potions to drink. At about 3.30 a.m. on 19th October I went to the loo and all the potions and pills worked their magic. I was so excited that at last something was going right that I woke Martin with squeals of elation. He came running into the bathroom bemused and alarmed only to see me sitting on the toilet whooping with delight. We laughed like banshees that night in the bathroom; I think we laughed as hard as we had cried only a few hours earlier.

Morning dawned and another day began. My blood pressure was still not great, and I was still very uncomfortable, but I was determined to get up and walk around. I was not going back in that wheelchair. I had to get myself strong so that I could regain some control. I felt that if I were strong then I would be able to pass on some of that strength to my babies, because right now they needed all the help they could get.

One of the midwives came to see me after breakfast that morning with a breast pump. I had thought that by expressing my milk to feed the babies I would feel as though I were doing something constructive. The breast pump worked a little like a milking machine used on a farm, before the milk became Unigate.

For twenty minutes I sat holding a plastic funnel over my nipple which was suctioned on by the sucking and blowing of the machine; my nipple when sucked was elongated to three times its normal length and then it was released. Through this action milk from the milk ducts was supposed to start flowing and then the milk was caught in a little bottle that was attached to the funnel via a plastic tube. The action of the machine was supposed to mimic the sucking action of a nursing child. After twenty minutes I turned off the machine to inspect the contents of the bottle, and to my utter dismay all I could see was a dribble of yellowy liquid not quite covering the bottom of the bottle. The nurse reassured me that this was perfectly normal and that the more I expressed, the more milk I would produce. She even collected the two and a half millilitres of yellowy liquid in a tiny little syringe and gave it to me to take up to SCBU to give to one of the babies through their nasal gastric tube (I hoped they were not too hungry because if they blinked they would miss that meal).

We spent the day going up and down to see our babies. Flowers were still arriving and the phone messages were constant. Nicholas was not very well, he had two chest drains and the doctors had paralysed him to stop him from fighting the ventilator. He was unable to maintain any long-term stability and his condition was poor.

Joshua was not doing so well either, and by the end of the day he was urgently needing a blood transfusion. We were told that the two of them would be having a brain scan in the morning to see what was going on.

In the other room Jodi and Benjamin were not causing quite as many problems, they actually both seemed stable and making progress. Going from one room to the other was like going from one world to another. The equipment was all the same, the doctors were the same and even the nurses looked the same, but in Nicholas's and Joshua's room it was quiet and humourless, everyone spoke in hushed voices, and when they looked at my boys there was sorrow in their eyes. They were all working so hard to try to make them better, and it felt then that they were on a downhill slope, but none of us were ready to admit defeat, not yet. In contrast in the other room, everyone was laughing and joking and completely optimistic, there was a feeling of jubilation in this room, these two babies, the smallest of the tribe, were stable and making steady progress. This was without a doubt our happy room.

The day ended again and I hadn't noticed its passing. I had lost track of time, the minutes seemed so long yet the hours passed so fast. Meal times came and went, and family and friends visited and called, but I don't remember seeing or speaking to any of them. They had become almost irrelevant, they could not understand my emotions, or what was happening to us, and they could not change the outcome, therefore I could not put any energy into making them relevant. They dissolved back into a world that was no longer mine. My world had become the sixth floor of the Portland Hospital, the world outside seemed to have vanished and all the feelings and emotions that were part of the outside world had seemed to have disappeared along with it. In their place was a new world, full of new feelings, a rollercoaster of emotions the like of which I had never experienced; I was able to laugh and cry almost at the same time, and feel elated and crushed within seconds of each other. I didn't want anyone to be part of my new world; my babies were mine and if I let anyone else in it would mean that I had to share them. I didn't know how long I would have them, but I did know that however long it was no one else was going to love them more than me.

CHAPTER 29

Thursday 20th October. Once again the sun rose and it went unnoticed. Martin woke and went straight up to the sixth floor to see the babies, whilst I tried to ignore the pain and discomfort in order to prepare myself for the day ahead.

I tried to express some milk, but only managed a few measly mls. Then I washed and tried my best to make myself look presentable; not an easy task, and also not very successful.

Martin returned from the sixth floor where, although they had had a relatively quiet night, some results had come through and the doctors had asked to see us as soon as possible. I don't really think that I thought too much about what was about to happen. I went through the motions of eating and carried on as if the impending meeting was just routine, and eventually Martin and I went upstairs, and I was wheelchair and tube free.

We were asked to take a seat in the nurses' office, and Dr Millett joined us soon after. I had not even said good morning to my children yet. As soon as the doctor walked into the room I knew that the day ahead was going to be long, heartbreaking and very traumatic. He told us that both Joshua and Nicholas had had a brain scan, and neither of the results was very positive. Joshua was extremely unwell; his brain scan showed extensive damage, his internal organs were failing, and they were doubtful that he would live another night, and even with maximum help Joshua would die at some time today.

We had no time to digest this because he then went on to say that Nicholas had stabilised during the night, and if they carried on giving him all the help that they could he had a chance of surviving. However, his brain scan showed that he had had a massive bleed into his brain (on a scale of one to five with five being the worst, his was a four). They had had a team meeting before we had arrived and felt that if he survived he would be severely disabled and he would have no quality of life. In their opinion we should give him minimum help and let him die. If he fought to stay alive then it would show that the damage was not as bad as they thought, but this scenario was extremely unlikely.

We had to make one of the hardest decisions of our life. If Nicholas had not been a quin we would not have even been considering the question. We would have kept him on maximum help and faced the consequences of his handicaps; he would have been loved and cherished and we would have made sure that he would have some quality of life. But lying in the next room were two babies who were stable and fighting and who had every chance of surviving this ordeal, and I could be going home one day with three babies, one of which had severe special needs, and requiring twenty-four hour attention. We also knew that Jodi would have some degree of difficulty, but we didn't know in what areas they would show themselves. We had to make the decision; we had to do the right thing for all the family. How bizarre that after all the years of wanting so desperately to call ourselves a family we now had to make the decision to let one of our members die. We made the choice, although we really had none, and Nicholas was put on minimum help.

Sobbing we went to our dying sons; we stroked and talked to them searching for signs that the diagnosis was wrong. They were so tiny and so innocent and their short lives had brought them nothing but pain; their little chests were being pumped with huge pressures and the noise surrounding their incubators must have been almost deafening. I wondered if they could hear it. No one could tell me that. I knew we had so little time left with them, yet there was nothing that I could do to make their last few hours easier. I was still so damned ill and my body just would not do what I wanted it to. I wanted to sit by them and take it in turns to hold their tiny hands, to whisper into their ears, to hold and stroke them, to spend their last hours sitting beside them, because every child needs their mummy, especially when they are not feeling well. Mummies are supposed to make their children feel better, but I couldn't; I couldn't do anything to help my boys, they were slipping away from me and I would never see them again and there was absolutely nothing I could do.

At nine that evening within seconds of each other Joshua and Nicholas died. I was there in the room, but I wasn't holding them. I wondered if my voice was the last voice that they heard. If their souls had gone to heaven knowing that I was their mummy. In the short time they were with me I loved them so much, I knew every detail of their faces and every inch of their bodies. I would never know their bodies free from bruises, but I would hold their memory in my heart forever, and through my other children they would live on.

At 10.30 that night I went home for the first time in ten weeks.

CHAPTER 30

I t was dark when I left the hospital and the world looked strange. I felt drained and emotionless. The enormity of our loss was too great to rationalise and it had all happened in such a short space of time even though it seemed that the last five days were an eternity. I had to find an emotional haven; everything kept changing and the only way I could deal with what had happened was to shut down. I had to put my grief and loss in a corner to be retrieved at a later date. It was the present and the immediate future that was now my priority, and grief is something from the past.

Everything looked so different. My home somehow didn't look like the home that I had left that late summer morning ten weeks ago. The season had changed and so had our lives. The summer past was one never to be forgotten, but it had passed and with it had so many of our hopes and dreams.

Miffi came bounding up the path to greet me and even she looked different. Her love for me, however, was as sincere as it always had been. I didn't remember the furniture being so big, or the house being so small. It felt as though I had been away for so many years and I was looking at the home I loved so much through stranger's eyes.

Martin made a cup of tea and settled me in an armchair whilst he went upstairs to unpack my bags. I had left a large amount of my stuff at the hospital, but we would pick that up in the morning. Mum and dad were with us and were staying to help look after me for a few days, and they sat with me and we chatted about unrelated irrelevant things, and my eyes were dry.

It was midnight before I climbed into bed. I slept on Martin's side because it was nearer the bathroom and there was more space for me to clamber in and out of bed. I was still very cumbersome and in a certain amount of discomfort.

At about two in the morning I awoke not knowing where I was. My bed didn't go up and down like it did in the hospital so it took me twice as long to sit up and get out of it, and it hurt a lot. I started panicking because there were no nurses to help me. I was so far away from my babies. What if they needed me there (which of course they wouldn't because there was really nothing that I could do for them, and I knew the hope that they knew that I was their mother was probably just that, a hope) and I couldn't get there in time? I eventually made my way across the tiny landing into the toilet, but I couldn't breathe properly, everything had changed so much. I felt as though I no longer belonged here. I needed to be home at the hospital where my children had lived and died. It was almost like I no longer belonged in this house. I was not the same person that had walked out the door all those weeks ago, and I knew that I never would be again; that person had died along with the little souls that were now in the bosom of the heavens.

My head started to feel light, and my chest couldn't take in enough breath. I stumbled back into the bedroom shaking and breathless, and woke Martin, who took one look at me and called the hospital. They were concerned that my blood pressure had risen and told me to return immediately. So in the dead of night I left my house to return home to where I had lived since the old me had disappeared.

Although my blood pressure was high, my symptoms were those of a panic attack and I was given a room for the night where I composed myself and calmed down. I slept for only a few hours and as soon as I woke I went to see Jodi and Benjamin. Dr Millet was examining them when I arrived and started to talk about Joshua and Nicholas, but we were in the happy room and I would not allow any sad talk in that room. It was at that moment that things suddenly took on a different meaning. Martin and I both became insanely superstitious. We would only speak about certain subjects in that room. Martin started holding open doors for people, and driving extremely courteously (very unusual for him) in the hope that one good deed deserved one back! We said prayers every day and kept the same routines, we felt that if anything we did changed too dramatically it would have a knock on effect and the stability and well being of our two remaining children would also change.

I went home that afternoon whilst it was still light, and my wonderful mother had made dinner for me and all Martin's family as well as my sisters. It was a Friday night and all the men went to pray at the synagogue. I lit the Sabbath candles for the first time since becoming a mother, and it seemed like I was engulfed in a dream world. How could the last few months have been real? Had I really given birth to five beautiful babies? Was it possible that three of them would never stand beside me whilst I blessed the candles? How could their destinies be so short? What kind of mother has no real tangible memories of her children, and how could anyone understand that my love for them was the same as they had for their own, when they didn't know them? No one had seen them or touched them, no one would ever be able to share in our grief or love for our precious gifts that were taken from us so soon. I stood in front of the candles and thought, how can I give thanks, yet how could I not. I searched into my soul to try to find my true belief, and thought that if I gave up now then perhaps something more might happen. Is it guilt that keeps us believing in God, or is it blind faith? What was it in those darkest moments that compelled me to carry on in my prayers? Perhaps I wanted to believe that somehow the innocent beautiful souls of my three boys were in a better, more pure place and that they would be happier than here in this world, because the thought of them going to nothing was and still is an unbearable notion.

CHAPTER 31

The weekend passed and Jodi and Benjamin remained stable. All our hopes were now pinned on these two tiny little beings who were both still fighting to remain stable, and they seemed to be succeeding.

I continued with my breast milk donations, but they were not increasing in quantity. My friend Jackie had lent me her steam steriliser so that I could sterilise all the components of the pump. For me this seemed like a normal activity for a new mother to be performing, and I savoured every minute because it was a positive and useful contribution and gave me a sense of control.

My telephone rang constantly with well-wishers and people wanting as much information as possible in order to pass it on to as many of their friends as they could think of. I later found out that we were suddenly the most popular people in the area; people we didn't even know were claiming to be our friend.

We went backwards and forwards to the hospital and took it in turns to sit next to our son and daughter. Martin had backed off from the children, he preferred to sit on a chair between the two of them and watch the monitors and play patience. This way if anything else happened to them he felt it wouldn't hurt so much because he had not allowed himself any bonding time.

I, however, wanted to do as much as possible for them. I changed their tiny nappies and washed their faces. I held their hands and stroked their perfect little faces. As each minute passed I fell more and more in love with them. They became little people, and they seemed to have different personalities. Benjamin frowned with concentration, yet seemed content to lie there and be tended to, whilst Jodi did not stop moving. Her arms waved and her legs kicked and she fought hard to stay alive and keep everyone on their toes. My heart swelled with this love, I had never known a feeling like it. These two people were my flesh and blood, together Martin and I had created them. They were going to grow up one day and have independent lives, they would be separate from us, with different views and opinions, and individual thoughts and ideas, and the miracle was that they were a part of us. The meaning of parenting had never been so real, and it was a wonderful miraculous feeling, and one that I felt truly privileged to have experienced.

We spent the weekend going backwards and forwards to the hospital. My dad brought my grandparents to see the babies; I wanted them to see the happy room. I still cannot imagine what they were thinking or how they were dealing with all that had happened. The strange thing is I remember them being there, but I don't remember any words, in fact I seem to have lost so many memories of that time. The four of us (Martin and the babies) were my world. We were in a bubble, and within the confines of the walls of that bubble we were safe, and so my recollections of life outside that space are a little disjointed.

Although I went to the hospital early in the morning, my health was still not as wonderful as I would have liked. So my mum would come and collect me during the day to take me home for a rest and also to allow me time to express my drips of milk.

On the way home on one of those days I had an overwhelming desire to drive the car. It was my car, my convertible, and I had not driven it for almost six months. Again it was a control issue. If I were driving I would be regaining some semblance of control and normality. Mum was not too happy, after all I was recovering from major surgery, and my blood pressure was still quite high. However, she did not feel she had the right to deny my request, so she pulled over onto the straightest stretch of road that she could find, and I climbed in behind the wheel and started to drive. I really don't know how to put into words the feeling of freedom I experienced in those moments. I felt as if the last six months were a dream, that this moment was reality. It was what normal people did every day, and I had regained some normality. For a moment my spirits were lifted and I felt as though one day our lives would once again become the same as everyone else's, just working, shopping, driving from place to place, and cooking and cleaning. I didn't know when that would be or what would happen between now and that time, but I knew that one day this time of our life would be a memory and we would move on to find some sense of peace.

We arrived home and I staggered into my house feeling exhilarated yet drained, and on hooking up to the breast pump realised that normal was not going to happen in the near future.

It is strange now how when looking back that I wanted "normal" so desperately when really there is probably no such thing as normal. One set of circumstances is just replaced by another and somehow after a while whatever we are dealing with at the time becomes our normal. It was a lesson I had yet to learn.

CHAPTER 32

The next few days were relatively uneventful. Dad returned to Brighton and mum stayed a while to nurse me back to health. Joanne took up residence in the box room, and life took on a surreal type of routine. Trips to the special care unit, postnatal checks, breast pump and rest at home became my life. I changed, talked, fed and stroked my children, and built up new relationships with the hospital staff. They were becoming our new family. Leaving the hospital to come home was a wrench, yet all I wanted was to be home.

Benjamin lay content and happy on his furry mattress happy to be pampered like any male. He almost purred when he was stroked and he happily accepted his feeds through his nasal gastric tube, filling his nappy regularly and enjoying all the attention that was being bestowed on him. The only time he became a little cross was when the physiotherapist banged away at his little chest or when the doctors came and stuck him with needles, then he would frown and wave his arms in protest, but only momentarily because once they had left his side he would lie back and relax again until the next time.

Jodi on the other hand was not so content to let the world go by; she was impatient to get on with her life. She moved around all day, fighting to pull out her various tubes and drains. She tossed her head from side to side and kicked her tiny little hands and feet. She kept the staff on their toes and soon became the focal point of the unit.

I loved them both so much and as each minute and hour passed my love grew. I could devote all my time and effort into studying each expression on their faces and every detail of their bodies. I didn't have to make up bottles or keep the house clean; I didn't have sleepless nights like other new mums. There were no distractions, my children had my total undivided attention, there were not even phone calls taking me away from their sides. The time I had with these children was so intense that each minute that passed was the equivalent of hours, and each day seemed like weeks. I could no longer remember a time when these two little mites were not here; I could no longer remember a time when my heart was not full of the love for them. Every thought in my head was of them and about them. As I opened my eyes in the morning I saw their faces and they were the last thought in my head as I fell asleep at night.

Ten days after the birth of my babies it was time to have my stitches removed. I had been going down to the third floor daily to have my postnatal checks, and also because my blood pressure was taking its time returning to normal. On the day in question, Martin dropped me outside the hospital and went off to park his car. On my way inside a young man opened the door for me and as I passed him he wished me luck! Well, he really was in the wrong place at the wrong time; my hormones rushed to my head and I yelled back in response that I had actually had THEM! And three of them had died and two were still fighting for their lives up in the Special Care Baby Unit! The blood drained from the poor man's face and he exited the hospital rather speedily. It wasn't until months later that I realised that my outburst was not completely necessary.

My stitches came out and although it wasn't the most pleasant of experiences it was not as bad as anticipated. After my legs had stopped shaking I managed to make my way back up to the sixth floor to tend to my offspring.

On the twelfth day after the birth we arrived at the hospital early, early being 7.30 in the morning. Martin liked to get there to see the doctors when they did the first rounds of the day. He always had so many questions to ask and they were invariably the same ones as the day before and more often than not the answers were the same. However, on this day it was different. On entering the unit we noticed that Jodi was no longer wearing her hat, she was lying in a head box and she was not attached to the ventilator. She was well enough to breathe without support. For the first time in her short life we were able to see her face. The shape of her tiny little rosebud mouth, her eyes open and searching, her fiery red hair, and her beautiful head and cheeks calling out to be touched and kissed. She looked so beautiful and although she was before, she seemed to be more real. I just wanted to go over and pick her up, to dress her in pretty baby clothes and lie with her next to me, and today for the first time I felt that one day that may become a reality. Benjamin on the other hand was stable and plodding along nicely, but with no sign of any change at the moment.

It all changed again on day fourteen. We were called in to the hospital even earlier than we usually arrived. On arrival we found that Jodi had been intubated again (they had put her back on the ventilator) and seemed to be causing some cause for concern. And in the other corner Benjamin was also not doing so well. They had given both children a lumbar puncture and they were both on large doses of antibiotics. It seemed that both of them had developed an infection.

Martin and I went downstairs for some fresh air and for the first time in nearly a year I lit a cigarette. I had no head rush, I didn't feel sick, I enjoyed every deep long drag, and thanked God that something could make me feel momentarily better. I decided at that moment that I needed the cigarettes more than Jodi and Benjamin needed the twenty-five millilitres of breast milk that I was able to produce each day. So the breast milk stopped and the smoking continued.

The day passed and the children seemed a little more stable by the time we left in the evening. Benjamin had been given a course of steroids, and Jodi had a drug to try and close a valve in her heart that was allowing the blood to flow backwards instead of forwards and therefore not taking enough oxygen around her body. They were both settled so we said our prayers for them, kissed them through the portholes of the incubators and went home.

Routine became paramount. We went the same way home in the evenings and the mornings, we listened to the same tape, we said the same prayers and never said anything unkind about anyone. Martin when driving became so considerate, letting other drivers in and out of traffic in front of him, which was totally out of character for him. We felt that if we did the same thing every day, and were good people, then maybe no more bad would happen to us. It is only when looking back that I realise how obsessive we had become.

CHAPTER 33

The days passed. Benjamin could never quite recover the ground that he had lost with the infection; he needed maximum help with everything, but fought the ventilator to the point that a decision was made to sedate him. We asked the same question over and over, "Is he going to live?" We needed comparisons of other babies that had been as sick and had made it home eventually. There were always comparisons with happy endings, and there were also not so favourable outcomes in the comparisons. We continued to pray and stay optimistic. I remember lying in bed during my fitful sleepless nights praying with all my heart, asking God to just look down this once and give these two innocent souls the strength to survive. Perhaps that was a selfish thing to do in view of the fact that there were already so many other souls for him to help, but I thought if he could just do one more miracle. On our journeys to and from the hospital we talked of the day when we would bring our babies home, of how as they grew Martin would take Benjamin to play football in the park and how Jodi would push her dolls pram. We imagined our life to be totally complete, and these thoughts gave us hope, so we held onto them and they became part of our ritual.

Jodi was back on the ventilator and seemed set to stay there. Although she was not on as much support as her brother, neither was she on minimum support. She gave the nurses and doctors a run for their money, every so often she would drop her heart rate and turn blue, and all the alarms would sound and we would watch with our hearts in our mouths. Because after losing the other boys we knew that life was so fragile and anything could happen at any time, this thought haunted us both every second of every minute of every day.

Although to us every day held different anguishes, joys, heartaches and hurdles, to recall everything would be impossible. We lived from one hour to the next waiting and hoping that the next blood gas taken from our children's veins would be the one that declared them better. Martin followed the doctors out to see the latest x-rays and listened intently to the diagnosis. He even started reading a medical encyclopaedia hoping to find a ray of hope within its pages.

The mornings dawned and the sun set, and we didn't notice because we couldn't see beyond the unit. Every evening we would come home and listen to an endless stream of messages on the answer phone, but we heard few. Joanne would always be home waiting for us, trying to be unobtrusive, but meek and mild was not in Joanne's nature and our house was very small.

Looking back life seemed impossibly hard, but I didn't notice because I was so focused on willing my babies better and everything else passed me by. And so it continued for a couple of weeks.

On Sunday 13th November 1988 we were woken at 6 a.m. by the phone. It was the hospital informing us that Benjamin was really unwell and we should make our way to the hospital as soon as possible. We dressed in minutes and were in the car and on our way within ten minutes of receiving the call. It took us seven minutes to drive the distance. Fortunately speed cameras had not yet been invented.

By the time we arrived at the hospital Benjamin had been stabilised, he was still on maximum help, but they thought that he may have had a mucus plug that had made it difficult for him to breathe and therefore sent all his readings haywire.

Meanwhile in the opposite corner Jodi seemed to be causing concern. There were doctors and nurses all round her and they all seemed to be prodding, bagging and pricking her. She was having problems maintaining her oxygen levels and her breathing was becoming more laboured. I became very emotional and one of the nurses pulled me over to see Benjamin, claiming that he was well now and that I should draw strength from this fact. It seemed quite ironic that for the first time since his birth he was the stronger of the two and it took such a dramatic turn on Jodi's part for him to achieve this status. Eventually both children were well enough for us to leave the hospital for a while and go home. Joanne had called both sets of grandparents at six that morning, and they had all driven up together from Brighton, so we all went back to our house at about two that afternoon.

I made everyone a cup of tea as soon as we arrived home and was about to start drinking mine when once again the hospital called to say that they were unable to stabilise Jodi and we should return immediately. So once again, leaving our cups almost full, we returned to the hospital.

We watched as the hospital staff worked to try and save our baby. No one was prepared to give up, least of all Jodi. They fought, and she fought and we prayed, smoked and cried, but eventually someone must have heard our prayers because they managed to stabilise her. She was back on maximum help, but she was alive.

Drained and exhausted we finally returned home. Mum and dad went back to Brighton with my in-laws and we poured ourselves a very strong stiff drink. It seemed that our babies were a long way from the edge of the woods.

CHAPTER 34

Although both the children were relatively stable we decided that we needed to spend as much time at the hospital as possible. We wanted to be there when the doctors did the early morning rounds and I felt that any time away from my babies was a waste; their time with me was precious and I was not sure if the next hour would be my last with them.

On 16th November 1988 we arrived at the hospital at our usual time to find four doctors standing over Benjamin talking in hushed tones and fiddling with the settings on his ventilator. They all looked very grave but not sad. As we approached, one of them looked up, and on realising that we had arrived, stepped away from the incubator and came to our side.

He explained to us that Benjamin had been on maximum help for much longer than they had hoped and the problem now was that if he had even a minor setback there would be nowhere for them to go, they were unable to give him any more help. So what they had decided to do was bring all his settings down and see if perhaps he was just being lazy and was actually able to do more by himself. It was now a waiting game, in half an hour they would take his blood and then from that they would be able to maintain if he was taking in enough oxygen and at the same time burning off the correct amount of carbon dioxide.

It was an endless half an hour but at the end of it they found that although he was well oxygenated he was building up his carbon dioxide levels and as a result they had to turn all his machines back up to maximum yet again.

The only problem was that he now had too much carbon dioxide in his blood and this for Benjamin was dangerous and toxic. It was going to be a waiting game to see if he could burn it off himself, because as mentioned before, there was nothing else the doctors could do to help; he was on the maximum of everything.

During this waiting game Martin and I realised that we had not yet registered any of the children's births and we were in fact running out of time. We needed to do that as soon as possible. So off we went to the place where you register births (different place from the registering deaths place).

The lady helping us struggled to grasp all the facts that we were presenting her with. We had had five children all at once and needed to register all of their births, and unfortunately three of our babies had not survived and their deaths had already been registered, and the two remaining babies were both in critical condition. I know that on repeating all these facts I should have been crying but for some reason my warped sense of humour took over at that moment and I started to giggle and had to wait outside, because the look on that poor lady's face was one of shock, sympathy and disbelief and all of that made me laugh; a little like when someone falls over or hurts themselves, I find that perversely amusing as well.

We left the registry office a while later and decided to pop home and have a quick bite of lunch. When we arrived, Jill and Philip came in to see us all depressed because she had just had a laparoscopy that showed that everything was normal and that meant that there was no apparent reason for her not to have fallen pregnant. I sat listening to her and then realised that I really wasn't in the right frame of mind to be counselling anyone else, not at this moment in time when my life was not really going as well as could be expected. So I excused myself and told them that we really had to be going back to the hospital because the children that we had fought so hard to bring into this world were in critical condition and I needed to be by their sides.

The traffic on the way to the hospital was dreadful and I felt very irritated by this. I had this sense that I needed to be back at the hospital urgently and I didn't really know why.

It took about an hour to get to the hospital and when we arrived things had taken a turn for the worse. Benjamin had been given drugs to paralyse him. He had been unable to burn off the carbon dioxide all day and the doctors felt that he had been fighting the ventilator, so the decision that they had all come to was that in order for him to have a chance of survival he was better off being paralysed. I knew then at that moment that things were very serious, and that there was a high probability that Benjamin may not survive the night. So I sent Martin to call our parents. They didn't say that he was not going to make it, but I knew from his brothers that once they had been paralysed and no longer had to work for themselves, they no longer were able to fight and it was as if they gave up the battle of life.

I looked at my son's face and he no longer had the little frown of concentration, his face was expressionless; it was like he had already started his journey to the sky. The night nurse took over and as Sandy, the day nurse, left she said to us that she had a good feeling about him and that his oxygen levels had been good all day and that was a good sign because it meant that his brain was still normal. The bizarre thing was that when Sandy spoke those words they were like a life line thrown to us in the depths of the sea. We clung to anything that would make these hours more bearable. To give up hope was unthinkable, even when we knew deep down that the worst was inevitable.

Good oxygen levels for our babies at that time were anything over about sixty, one hundred being the best and zero the worst. We went down to have a cigarette at about 7.30 and his oxygen levels were about seventy. Twenty minutes later we returned and they were eight.

Our boy was slipping away and I had never even seen his face without a tube. He was a month old and I didn't really know what he looked like. I told the nurse that this time I wanted to hold my baby for his last minutes, I wanted his tubes removed and I wanted to take him in my arms so just once in his very short life he would know the comfort of his mother's arms. I don't think he felt my tears on his face as I willed and prayed so hard for him to breathe on his own whilst I held him for that very last time, but he had had enough. He was going to a better place now, with his brothers where he belonged, to a place where he would not be stuck with needles or prodded and poked; he would finally be at peace and his pain would be no more.

Our fourth baby boy died at 9.30 p.m. on 16th November 1988. Our hearts were broken and I couldn't imagine how they could ever be repaired. Our daughter lay fighting and critical and alone. In such a short space of time we had loved enough for an eternity and the grief of our loss would last for longer.

I couldn't imagine feeling happy again, or waking up in the morning without that terrible sinking feeling as consciousness took over; the realisation that the dream world that I had scarcely left was just that, a dream, and in actual fact our life had become a trauma. To wake to that feeling of plunging into the depths of despair yet trying so hard to pull through it and hold onto a glimmer of strength and swim up to some sort of light. I couldn't imagine surviving this yet neither could I imagine not.

I left him his teddy to take with him when they came to take him to his brothers and after that day another prayer never passed my lips.

CHAPTER 35

Our parents arrived soon after Benjamin had died, but I really don't remember too much about them being there. I remember Stanley (my father-in-law) tried to take him away before I was ready to give him up and I remember feeling very angry with him. The only thing I remember clearly was that I felt the most enormous sense of loss. It was almost disbelief that I would never see my son again, that when I came tomorrow he would no longer be here, and I would never feel that immense surge of love that used to overcome me when I saw his little face and helpless little limbs. The knowledge that I would never dress him nor change his nappy, never see again the irritation in his eyes when the physiotherapist banged on his little chest or the look of satisfaction when his milk was passed through his tube satisfying his hunger, or the frown of concentration when he was being stabbed with needles as if he were trying to block out the pain. I couldn't imagine never seeing any of those things again. I felt empty, as though my soul were being drained. I felt myself shutting down, because I think that was the only way that I could cope with the emotional trauma of the last month. I remember thinking how much more could one endure before breaking, and I wondered if we would have to find out for ourselves. I left the hospital that night a different person. All the praying, the superstitious routines and the blind belief in a greater power had left my heart. I felt there was no point to any of it, to watch my children fighting so hard to live, to have spent their short time on this earth connected to tubes and drips, never to experience pleasure, sunshine, rain and snow, to never know a mother's embrace and know only pain and suffering, for what ... to be taken away to darkness and strangers. How could I ever give thanks again? How could I ever praise the Lord or tell God that I loved him unconditionally? If there were in fact a higher power what kind of lesson was it trying to teach? If there was a lesson in our sons' suffering it was one I didn't want to learn.

I couldn't say goodbye to either of my children that night. The nurse took Benjamin from me and I left the unit without looking back. My heart was breaking and I didn't know how it would or could ever mend.

The next day we returned to the hospital resolved to be optimistic for Jodi. She would not know our sorrow or feel our despair, we would be strong for her and fight for her with courage and strength, and whilst I truly believed that our resolve was purely for her, I now believe that it was my way of dealing with an emotionally impossible situation. I was fighting for my survival as much as for hers. She had a long road ahead if she was going to live and we had to be there to help and encourage every single step of the way. And so we put on our happy faces and together in our determination to continue positively we took the lift to the sixth floor where our last remaining GIFT lay fighting for her life.

The nurses and doctors all gave us sympathetic greetings and we accepted them as politely and gracefully as we could, and then we went to be with our girl. She wasn't doing so well either. Her heart rate kept dropping as did her oxygen levels. She was back on maximum help from all the machinery and every hour on the hour the doctor would take her blood to test her various levels, and they were not looking as good as they had been. Every so often she would turn a shade of blue and the nurse would end up bagging her with a special bag that administered the oxygen into the lungs with more pressure and more precision. Eventually she would stabilise for a while until the next episode.

More tests were requested, different blood screening, brain scans, and a heart scan. We then waited again for more results. During all of this a rabbi from the burial society came to take Benjamin and I made the decision not to see him one last time before he was taken away forever. It was a decision I would live to regret. From that day I felt that I should have said one last goodbye, but no amount of goodbyes could ever have been enough, the grieving process was one that I was beginning to become quite familiar with, and what I have learnt is that this process is never over, it just becomes part of one's life, and the person grieving has to decide how to use it. I gave Martin Benjamin's special teddy with instructions that it stayed with him, he was not to be put in the ground without it, and then I let him go, but I knew his flame would burn in my heart for the rest of my life.

Eventually Jodi's results arrived. There was a valve in her heart that should have closed at birth. Its function was to stop the blood going back into her system before it was oxygenated. The doctors had tried to close it using drugs when she was only a week old, but it seemed to have opened again and that meant that some of the blood going round her little body was not carrying any oxygen. Consequently she was not receiving enough oxygen to her brain and organs, hence the attacks of turning blue and her dropping heart rate and oxygen levels.

The solution was closed heart surgery. They would have to take her to theatre and open her chest and close the valve using a pin. A simple routine procedure if the child was a robust seven-pound full term baby, and not a critical preterm very sick child like ours. However, we had no choice; without the operation she would die. With the procedure she had a fifty-fifty chance of survival. The surgery was scheduled for the next evening. Once again our parents were called and once again early the next morning they arrived at the hospital to face another day of uncertainty.

They took Jodi down for surgery at eight o' clock in the evening. She was wrapped in silver foil like a chicken ready for roasting. I sat with my parents, in-laws and husband in the relatives' room, and for the first time in my life I lit a cigarette in front of my mother and I made no apologies.

It seemed like an endless amount of hours before they brought our baby back, and I actually don't remember how long she was gone, but she came back alive and pink and fighting. This child had absolutely no intention of giving up this fight. Her brothers were together, but she was staying put. They were her guardian angels, and still are to this day. They were going to watch over her and protect her, and she would do everything in her power to stay on this earth and live a long and happy life. There was no doubt about her will to live that night, and for the first time in her short life I was proud of her. I was proud of her determination and stubbornness. This child was a tough cookie and her character would help her through some very tough milestones in the future, and as for me, this tiny ray of sunshine had set alight a flame in my soul which would help and guide me through my grief and sorrow, even if it couldn't extinguish it, it was my comfort.

CHAPTER 36

The next couple of days were pretty much uneventful, then two days after her surgery we came in to find Jodi in a head box and without her ventilator tube attached. She had the sweetest tiny little face with a shock of bright red hair, and a minute nose and rosebud mouth. She looked like a real baby, kicking and waving her limbs in uncoordinated oblivion. For the first time in months I felt a glimmer of optimism, and silently hoped that this was perhaps the turning point, that maybe this was the corner the doctors kept talking about.

It was like being given hope with one hand however, and then in the next moment the other hand took it away, for after only a few hours Jodi developed an infection which affected her breathing, and she was soon back on the ventilator again.

For some reason I didn't go to pieces, I just felt in my heart that somehow she would get through this, and it was just another setback. Naturally, I felt great disappointment and frustration, but I could be patient; the doctors and nurses had seen her through worse than this and I knew that they would not let me down this time.

It was a rough couple of days, but she eventually stabilised; however, she was still ventilated and still required a high level of support. Day after day the doctors would come and see us, and day after day Martin would ask the same questions: When would we see an improvement? Why was it taking so long? Would she live and will she ever come home? The list went on and on, but there were no answers; no one knew for sure what the future held for our little girl, her life was in the balance. As each day passed she was gaining strength, but any unusual virus or bacteria could have had a devastating effect. So the doctors answered with patience and a relative amount of understanding, but never committed themselves to a long-term prognosis.

The next few weeks were a rollercoaster of emotions and changes. One day we would come in and Jodi was requiring less help and seemed pink and settled, the next hour she could suddenly change and be on maximum help, with a blood transfusion, sedated and needing antibiotics. We never knew what to expect, and each day would bring new anxieties. However, the hospital and all the staff were becoming our life, and although we saw our very closest friends on the odd occasions that we were home or they popped in to see us at the hospital, I didn't answer calls anymore and I certainly had no inclination to see people that were not directly involved with our life.

We had become institutionalised. Martin had a thick red beard and refused to shave until we were sure that Jodi was going to live, and he spent hours and hours in the hospital playing patience and reading the rather large medical journal, trying to understand Jodi's condition as best he could. He followed the doctors when they took blood gases and read her x-rays listening for any sign of hope, and he questioned everyone endlessly hoping that by some miracle they could give him an answer that was different from the hour before when he had asked the exact same question to a different member of staff.

One doctor told us to look for changes over a longer period of time, for example, don't try to see a difference from yesterday, but try to see a difference from two weeks ago, and I suppose there was a gradual improvement, but it was so gradual, it could be easily missed.

In the middle of December, when Jodi was still being very gradual in her improvement, it was decided to bring in a specialist from Great Ormond Street Hospital to see if maybe he could shed some light on why Jodi did not seem to be making very much headway. After considering all her notes and looking through her x-rays, and of course giving her a very thorough examination, he told us that Jodi was going to live, and that it may take a while but she would come off the ventilator and one day she would come home. He couldn't give us a time frame, but we had heard what we had wanted to hear for such a long time: our baby was going to survive, and we would see her first smile and watch her grow and have her in our home where we could love and cherish her for the rest of our lives. He had given us the greatest gift in the world, he had given us hope, and now it didn't matter how long, we could wait for however long it was to take. That night when Dr Millet came to see Jodi, he asked Martin if he had any questions, and when Martin said "No" Dr Millet began banging his head against the wall. It was an amusing moment, for after all these months, one visit from another doctor and Martin no longer had any questions or worries. He now knew that one day his little girl would be coming home and so all the questions and answers in the world were at this moment in time irrelevant. They no longer mattered, because they could not change anything. She would live to come home and that was that.

That night Martin shaved his beard and decided to return to work. However, before he did we went to John Lewis and spent some serious money on our child. We bought lacy sheets and tiny baby grows, little vests and mobiles, the smallest crib bumpers we could find, and little teddies. We took them all back to the hospital where we dressed her incubator with all her new acquisitions. It was the prettiest incubator the nurses had ever seen in the Special Baby Care Unit. For us to see her dressed in clothes, all be it they were rather large for her, and to see her surrounded by baby things and not only tubes and syringes made her more real. It was as though she was transformed from a tiny suffering animal to a real baby. It didn't mean that we loved her more because things surrounded her; it just made our parenthood more of a reality. In a way we had some control over our child and her future, even if it was only the decision of what colour sheet to wrap her in.

Although she had not yet turned her corner, we had turned ours. We knew that it was not going to be a smooth journey, but we also knew that one day we would be waving goodbye to the sixth floor of the Portland Hospital, but until that day arrived we had to be patient and enjoy as many pleasures of parenting a child on a special care unit as was possible.

CHAPTER 37

The days and weeks passed and our daily routine changed marginally from day to day, and whilst we struggled with our life as it was, Jodi continued with her steady progress, and the nurses adored her and fought to look after her.

We would bring in cakes and bagels and other goodies on a weekend and the nurses and doctors would enjoy all that they were given. Soon they became our friends and the hospital our new home, so much so that I could not imagine a time when this life would change. How strange the difference in my life in such a short space of time. Only a year ago I believed that I was infertile and yet here I was a mother of five and grieving for four, and in those months when I couldn't imagine being pregnant my life didn't seem set to change. How naïve was I to think that things would stay the same. It is a lesson that I have taken with me always since. Life is about change.

On Christmas Eve, 1988, we came in to find that Jodi had been extubated; she was no longer attached to the ventilator and was breathing alone in a head box once again. We had planned to go out for the evening with some friends and a couple of the nurses, but felt loathed to leave Jodi. I always felt that her progress would be faster if I were around. I am sure that were not the case at all, but it was a way of thinking that helped me to cope with my helplessness. However, I was persuaded to leave her for a few hours to go and have some normal entertainment.

Sitting in the restaurant with all our closest friends on Christmas Eve had in the past been a fairly normal event, but now for the first time we were out and we had other responsibilities. We were parents and our daughter was on the road up a mountain and some time in the coming year she was going to reach the summit. That night we drank champagne in between calling the hospital every hour to make sure that Jodi was still off the ventilator, and that her breathing was not too fast nor too slow, and that her colour was still good, and that she had had no set backs, and every hour we were told the same thing, and that was that she was stable and doing well.

That night Jodi turned her corner, from here on in she would go from strength to strength. Our next battle now, however, was to get her breathing air and out of the head box. This was to prove to be quite a difficult task, because what we didn't know until now was that oxygen was addictive and she had to be weaned off it like any addict that was trying to get rid of their habit.

Within a couple of days Jodi was able to drink small amounts from a bottle, and I was able to feed her. She always seemed so alert and busy, trying to absorb all her surroundings and the new sensations of being handled and bathed, and I was beginning to feel like a real mummy. I was able to bath her and change her, then wrap her in a soft blanket and hold her while she took hours to drink twenty mls of formula milk out of a bottle.

I had never experienced a love like this one and every day it grew. It was all consuming and permeated every bone in my body; my heart was so full that I couldn't imagine that there could ever be room for anything else. My daughter would lie in my arms attached to tubes and monitors oblivious to all of them because she had never known anything different, yet as I held her she was content, settled and alert and absolutely perfect. Sometimes she would fall asleep whilst I was holding her and I would sit there embracing her and revelling in the contentment of the moment. My life was her, nothing else mattered, and for the first time in years I felt happy and whole, and marvelled at the fact that such a tiny thing could summon such a range of emotions.

Life on the sixth floor continued and we had a little clan of parents with long-term special care babies. Although it was a way of life that we could not imagine changing, we were all living for the day that we would be told that we were going home with our babies. But the days passed, and although Jodi was growing steadily she was still in oxygen, and was very dependent on it. Martin would stand by her cot, and if the monitors showed that she had 100 per cent oxygen in her blood, he would turn down the oxygen being administered. However, within a few minutes he would be forced to turn it back up when Jodi went a dusky shade of blue around the mouth.

All was going well. Jodi was moved out of the special care unit and into the nursery. She was having periods of time where she was receiving no oxygen and although she wasn't able to stay out permanently, she was going for increasingly longer stretches. It was decided that before Jodi came home we should go to Bart's hospital to learn how to resuscitate her if the need arose at home. We would also need a suction machine and other equipment to ensure that should anything happen when we finally brought her home we would have everything to hand. We were also going to have to bring her home in oxygen, so I arranged with the local chemist to be on standby to deliver a large oxygen cylinder and a portable one, and they would be filled, as was required.

We had a beautiful nursery made for her and one of the nurses made her curtains, because everyone on the special care unit had formed a unique and extraordinary attachment to our precious daughter who had spent so many months fighting to survive, melting the hearts of all that cared for her, and so they all wanted a part in her recovery, even if it was to simply make a pair of curtains. We ordered her crib and carrycot, a car seat and changing mat. I found the tiniest clothes, which cost a fortune, but I didn't care. I felt like I was dreaming, and although it seemed the most natural progression of events, I couldn't come to terms with the journey that we had travelled in order to get here.

So many tears had been shed, so many hours waiting and praying, so much uncertainty and yet after all this we were preparing for the homecoming of our most precious gift, the gift that I had prayed so hard for and now after all the heartbreak and all the worry we were finally going to bring our daughter home.

A few days before we were to bring Jodi home she did something that would shape the way for her future. She did what no one expected her to do: she stopped needing the oxygen. Even Dr Millett was surprised and we were over the moon. We would still need to have the oxygen at home, but we would only need it occasionally if at all.

On 23rd February 1989 I spent the night with my daughter for the first time in a room on my own at the Portland Hospital. She was twenty weeks old and this would be the last night of the first part of her journey into the world. I sat on my bed with her lying on my knees looking at me, and as I sang her a lullaby she smiled a proper smile, not wind nor a grimace but a proper, real happy smile, and I cried.

The next day I took my baby home, and at that moment it was the best day of my life so far. Whilst my journey and hers was only just beginning we had already climbed a range of mountains, and with each setback and emotional crisis I had somehow recovered even though I am sure with each episode a little part of me changed forever. I am not saying that this was not a good thing, because I would not be the person I am today if I had not been on the journeys that I had travelled during those months. When I left the hospital that day I felt I was leaving a part of my soul behind, and although it was without a doubt a wonderful happy day it was also my saddest. How could emotions be so intertwined, and how difficult is it to define which is which? As I carried my baby through the doors of the hospital, waving goodbye to all the wonderful nurses, doctors, and staff who over the last few months had become our family, crying, laughing, hoping and praying with us, I realised that our journey was somehow also theirs, and for every tear I shed they also shed their own, and for every moment of hope that I encountered they somehow felt that moment too, and so the bond I felt with them all is one that I came to realise would never be extinguished.

CHAPTER 38

It was quite a homecoming. My mum had sent an arrangement of daffodils, one for every day that Jodi had been in hospital. All the family were at home waiting for us, even my grandparents were there (who I am sure often wondered if they would ever get to see the day they would be able to hold their great-grandchild). I don't remember the weather, and I don't even remember the journey home, I just remember saying goodbye to what I had now come to consider my second home, and bidding farewell to all the staff and nurses who had become firm friends, and then I was home. In my own four walls with my husband and child, and my family all around us.

I thought I would feel nervous or apprehensive about bringing home this baby that had been so sick and was so tiny, but all I felt was joy and elation. This was what I had dreamed of for as long as I could remember. This minute little bundle was our future and I had absolutely no doubt in my mind that I could look after her properly and that she would become a ray of sunshine in everyone's life.

Sometimes a cloud would pass over me during those first months at home with Jodi, when I would allow myself to ponder over the loss of my beautiful boys. I would often dream that there was another floor of the hospital full of light and life, and when I went up there my baby boys would be lying side by side wrapped in white blankets, and I would wake up weeping. But most of the time I kept my grief deeply buried and concentrated on the happiness and hope that Jodi brought to every day.

I was determined not to wrap her up in cotton wool, and even more determined not to be overprotective or neurotic, so although she was extremely small and needed to wear a breathing monitor wherever she went and have an oxygen canister under her pram just in case she turned a shade of blue, we went everywhere. No one could hear her cry because the ventilator had damaged her vocal chords, so when I spoke to a pram that was doing nothing but bleeping in time to her breathing, telling it to, "Shh, stop crying we will soon be home", I did attract some very curious looks! But I was so proud. In my mind there was not another child in the world that was as special and precious as my daughter; she was a living miracle and nothing nor no one could ever take that away from me.

After having had no fresh air for twenty weeks of her life I made sure that I made up for it now Jodi was home. I would wrap her up well, no matter what the weather, and take her for walks with the dog, and no matter what the temperature outside she would sleep in the garden for at least an hour a day. The only problem with that was, because her cry could not be heard and I needed to be able to hear the bleeping of the monitor, I had to always have the back door open and be doing something in the kitchen. So whilst she was wrapped up against the weather I used to be very cold for a lot of the time. Still it was a sacrifice I was prepared to make; she had a lot of fresh air time to catch up on.

The time passed and it was soon time to take Jodi for her first out-patients check up with Dr Millett. It was our first big outing since she had come home, and we collected Martin on our way. Dr Millett was absolutely delighted with her progress, and I knew that Jodi would always hold a special place in his heart. He sent us to see a special doctor for her eyes, because sometimes babies that have been in oxygen for long periods do have problems with their vision, but she was fine although she would need monitoring for the next few years.

When we were told that she would need to be seen in six months I couldn't imagine how our life would be in six months. I had become so used to thinking and living from day to day that I had almost forgotten how to plan and think ahead to the future. In fact, I think it was more that I was afraid to plan for the future, because one thing I had learnt in the past year is you just never know what the next day is going to bring.

During those first weeks I also went to see Mr Smith so that he could check that I was healing properly and that all had gone back to where it should be. We briefly discussed the possibility of another baby, and he thought that it would be unlikely that I would fall pregnant without help, but for the next couple of months I should be careful just in case he were to be wrong, as my body would not be able to cope with another pregnancy so soon after the enormity of the last one. We also decided that I would return at the end of the year to discuss the possibility of having GIFT again.

All was ticking along nicely and our life soon fell into the category of almost normal. We started socialising again, and my days were filled with doing mummy things. Jodi had continuous checks and was seen by both physio and occupational therapists on a regular basis, but that for us was normal, it just slotted in to our daily life. I began having play dates with other mums in the area and my life became all I dreamed it would be.

My health visitor Fran came every week to weigh and monitor Jodi and would have a cup of tea and a chat. On the day we decided to introduce solids into Jodi's diet I made sure Fran was there and had all the life saving equipment to hand. Thankfully, none of it was needed and the equipment went back into the cupboard unused.

In June Jodi weighed in at ten pounds and we almost had a party. She was the happiest sweetest little baby. She rarely cried and had a smile for everyone. Whoever she met fell in love with her. She filled my days with laughter and purpose, and filled the world with joy. I do believe that good always outweighs bad and during those first months after Jodi came home my belief was reinforced. It seemed that the losses and grief that I had encountered were sent to make me understand life differently. Up until then I suppose my life had been quite closeted in comparison to others, and now I understood so much more the complexities of emotions and valued the strength of character needed to progress and move through life in a constructive way.

By the end of the summer I was noticing that her development was not progressing at the same rate as some of my friends' babies, and Jewish mothers being what they are were very quick to compare their children. Most of the time I was so wrapped up in the joy that my baby was living and breathing that I didn't really notice the competition going on around me, but occasionally I would stop and think about it and get a little frustrated that Jodi was not sitting unaided or crawling or saying her first words. But then I would blame it on her start and convince myself that sooner or later she would catch up. And still she continued with her therapists.

In the Jewish religion a year after the death of a relative we have a stone setting. This is where there is a special service and the stone is put on the grave and relatives and friends go to say their last goodbyes.

We decided that we would have one stone for all the boys, and that we would make it known to our friends and family that there would be a small service to commemorate that they had lived.

It was a grey day at the beginning of September, but so many of our friends and family had come to support us and to say goodbye I was quite overwhelmed. The stone had the names of our boys and the dates each one was born and the date they died. Seeing it in front of me written for the world to see brought every moment of their short lives back to me, and suddenly they were real again, and I felt the terrible pain of the grief and loss flood back into my heart. I silently said goodbye to them and promised them I would never forget them as long as I lived and that even if it were for just one second every day, forever more I would think of them. The rabbi read out their names and as he did so the cloud broke and a beam of sunlight lit up the stone. At that moment I knew I was pregnant.

As I stood at the graveside of my beautiful sons reliving the grief and despair of the loss, I remembered each of their tiny little faces and bodies, their smell, and sensation of their skins, and my chest was filled with the same sorrow. It almost seemed as though time had actually not moved and that I was somehow back in the hospital at their sides and my tears seemed the same, and yet somehow I had managed to survive this first year; I could still smile and get pleasure from life, I could still feel the joys that were brought by my precious daughter, and I was still able to lie next to my husband in bed and feel pleasure from his touches. How strange that through all the grief and pain I was able to continue my life and to a stranger in the street I looked the same as everyone else, in spite of the fact that I felt so completely different. And now I felt the fluttering of new hope as I knew beyond all doubt that inside me grew the beginnings of a new life.

CHAPTER 39

When Jodi was still very tiny and very sick just after she had been born, I said to Martin that I would swap all our money and our wonderful lifestyle if only she would live. I suppose someone was listening, because the property market had crashed and there was a recession and we were no longer able to spend money the way we had been in the last few years. Martin had left his job and was now selling classic cars with a friend, and he worked from home which was not so great because he spent his life telling me to be quiet, and go out. It was to his advantage that Jodi's cry was almost inaudible. However, I was so blissfully happy with my new status as mother and mother-to-be that I wasn't bothered by our lack of funds in the slightest.

My values had changed; I had experienced life and death in such a concentrated space of time that I no longer put credence on materialism. So when Martin told me he had seen a job advertised in the *Estates Gazette,* because we were in fact running out of money fast and furiously I said fine and continued with making up bottles, then put it out of my mind.

Jodi's birthday was fast approaching, and with it came a mixture of extreme emotions. I was revelling in motherhood and so proud of her amazing achievements. She was almost sitting up unaided and would commando crawl across the floor, she sat in her high chair for meals and smiled and cooed and giggled from morning till night. Unless of course she hurt herself or was frightened by a loud noise, and then she would cry and be sick! Fran came every week to weigh her and she was slowly putting on weight. She was now almost eleven pounds.

When I went to the supermarket I would sit her in the trolley with a blanket tied around her middle to stop her slipping sideways (in those days they only had the one type of shopping trolley). Every time I went people would stop me to give me advice on how unwise it was to put such a young baby in the trolley, and I would very curtly reply that she was almost a year and it was in fact none of their business. How dare anyone comment on the way I was bringing up my daughter and in my mind I was the best mother to have ever walked the face of the planet. Looking back, however, it must have looked extremely odd to the outside world, for I had a child that was smaller than a baby of three months sitting up in a shopping trolley. I suppose all those people thought it was their duty to point out the error of my ways. None of them expected the reaction they received.

Jodi had three birthday parties, one for her friends, one for only family and one for my parents' friends. Her birthday cards lined the walls of the house and presents were in abundance. If someone had predicted this last year we could not have imagined it happening. I was now pregnant with my sixth child, and although I was very sick and very tired all of the time I felt as though this time it was the easiest thing that I had ever done. I was so happy I didn't notice how ill I was feeling.

On the anniversaries of our sons' deaths I lit and still light a special candle and to this day I cry as I bless them with a prayer meant only for them. Whatever milestone Jodi has reached I always imagine how it would have been with five, and even today I feel I have been cheated of those moments. It is a sadness that is part of my soul but with it I have learnt how to be happy and love my life and live every moment with optimism and energy. I had jumped so many hurdles to get this far that nothing would ever stop me enjoying and making the most of every hand I was dealt.

So Jodi's birthday came and went and soon after I announced to a shocked world that I was pregnant again, and I think the reaction was much the same as the first time. Everyone was delighted for us. The only one small problem was that we were very poor and were running out of money very rapidly. The classic car business was not really one that Martin was cut out for and he was getting a little concerned.

Then one day I was at the Portland Hospital with Jodi, who was having some physiotherapy, when the phone rang in the room and it was Martin telling me that he had been offered a fantastic job working for someone who was paying him to set up a residential investment portfolio. The new employer had had no experience in property and was paying Martin to set up a company the way he saw fit. It was a wonderful opportunity for Martin and he was delighted. I had reservations; I couldn't pinpoint why, it just seemed too good to be true and who was this man, we knew absolutely nothing about him. How did we know it wouldn't all end in tears? But at that moment in time we had no choice, there was no alternative, and besides that story will have to be left for another book in another time. Suffice to say, however, we were no longer poor and we no longer had to worry about the next penny at least for the next ten years anyway!

With new employment and new baby in mind, we sold our beautiful dolls house home and instead bought a house that needed absolutely everything doing to it. Whilst the works were being carried out my little family moved in with my wonderful mum and dad. All of a sudden I became my parents' little girl again yet this time around I was also a mother. Quite an identity crisis, and my mum being the person that she is finds standing back and allowing personal growth for her children quite difficult. Even today she has an opinion about everything that I do. It is usually not the way she would do it, and she does take umbrage if I don't take her advice on board, and in those days when I was in her opinion such an inexperienced mother I needed all the advice that she could muster. It didn't help that I had a cocktail of strange hormones raging around my body and sometimes her constant tips were not met with the most gracious of responses. Mind you I think that never changed even without the hormones! Nevertheless, once again the tides were changing, it seemed we were about to embark on yet another phase of our life.

CHAPTER 40

Our new house was being renovated and Jodi continued to bring joy to all who knew her. My parents were in their element having us around with all that came with us, and my stomach was swelling fast and furiously with the life of our new baby. Martin started his job, although there was a slight hiccup over contracts before he began and it nearly all went seriously wrong, but it was resolved and I just became more convinced that my husband's employer was not ever to be trusted.

We moved into our new home in the middle of December, and Jodi started coughing that day. We had been warned before she came home from hospital that she didn't have full lung capacity, but as she grew the healthy lung would be more than the damaged lung, but at this point in her life the damage to her lungs was significant.

I took her to the doctor and he said that her chest was clear and that there was nothing to worry about at the moment. As the day progressed her coughing became worse and her breathing became more rapid and more laboured. Once again I called the doctor, but it was after surgery hours and we had to call an emergency service and wait for the doctor to call us back. We still had not heard anything two hours later so we called again, to be told that the doctor had been trying to phone but there was a fault on the line so had given up. I demanded a visit as soon as possible and another two hours later the doctor arrived at our front door. He listened to her chest and still claimed that there was nothing to worry about. It was the middle of the night by now and I was tired and she was exhausted so I lay next to her in my bed and dozed in between coughing fits and clearing up sick and timing my little girls breathing whilst waiting for morning.

When morning finally arrived, it was with relief yet trepidation. Jodi was no better and if anything she was slightly worse. So back to the doctor we went to be told that she needed to be hospitalised. Our GP called Dr Millett and we met him at the Portland Hospital yet again. I was absolutely mortified; I knew that there was always going to be a chance that we would have to return to hospital for something, but I liked to believe that as her mother I would be able to protect her from that eventuality. It was like anything, although you know it is likely that if you smoke you will get cancer you don't actually expect to get it, you think that you will be the lucky one. It was the same in this case. However, here we were back at the Portland Hospital, and back on the sixth floor, but thankfully not in intensive care.

Jodi was becoming more and more lethargic and her breathing was becoming increasingly more rapid and she was really struggling. She was put straight onto a nebuliser, which is a machine that administers medicine via a mask over her mouth and nose. She was not impressed at all and kicked up a bit of a fuss, which was actually a really good sign, because if a child is very sick they have no energy to do anything, not even cry. All the monitors went back on and she was put back in oxygen. She had to have a chest x-ray and was put on oral antibiotics and steroids. The only problem with that was Jodi had a problem swallowing the foods that she liked, so trying to get her to take medicines without vomiting was almost impossible.

I think they may have had to change the carpet in that room after we had left because our daughter was so sick that day, and it was always unpredicted. The next day she was no better and really made no attempt to even lift her head so it was decided that they would have to put a drip into her to administer the antibiotics intravenously. She didn't flinch and I knew then that she was really quite unwell. It took a week, but true to Jodi's style she recovered almost instantly. One minute she was lying on the bed heavy eyed and unmoving and then suddenly she seemed to wake up and was crawling up and down the corridors laughing and flirting with anyone that would give her some attention. The dramatic change was incredible. In the morning I couldn't imagine sleeping in my own bed for at least another week, yet by the afternoon we were on our way home with a child that was as vivacious and lively as any other child her age.

This became her pattern. She would get a cough or cold more often when she was cutting a tooth. She would be admitted to hospital because she really was quite unwell and then she would recover so quickly that even the doctors were taken by surprise. Occasionally she would be quite unwell and the only way the doctor would believe us would be when they timed her heart rate and breathing rate, because she had the ability to stay active whilst most other children in the same situation would be in intensive care. Her resilience was incredible and she would only give up when she really had no alternative.

I, in the meantime, tried my very best not to be a neurotic mother, but I always had a thermometer to hand and would find myself timing her breathing at different times of the day just to make sure all was well. My days were filled with her, and her days were filled with activity, stimulation and loads of attention. Her friend Daniella would come every day with my friend Debbie, and we would sit and eat copious amounts of food whilst playing with our firstborns and planning for the arrival of our second children that were growing fast and furiously inside our bellies.

My life seemed perfect; it felt as though I had everything my heart desired, a lovely home, a beautiful little girl and another baby on the way. Martin was earning money, and even with our regular trips to the hospital for different therapies and check ups and the occasional admission for chest infections, it seemed as though I was cruising along with the perfect life. Even knowing that she was not developing at the same rate as her peers could not deter me from my feeling of contentment.

As my due date drew nearer I had to face the prospect of leaving Jodi with my parents for the duration of my hospital stay. I was having another caesarean as my uterus would not be strong enough to cope with a normal labour, having been stretched beyond capacity the first time round. I also worried about how I would be able to love another baby as much as I loved Jodi. I was so consumed by her that I couldn't imagine that there could be anything left for another baby. My mum, however, reassured me that what I was feeling was in fact perfectly normal and that all would be fine. Jodi would be okay without me for a few days and as soon as I held my new baby I would realise that the love one holds in their heart is infinite.

The birth of my sixth child was planned. I knew exactly what day, date and time it was to be born. The day before, I took Jodi to the hospital for some therapy and they told me that it was highly unlikely that she would walk before she was two and a half, which meant that there was a possibility that she would not learn to walk before her younger sibling. I buried that concern and went up to my room to be admitted. Mum and dad came to collect Jodi and I gave her a big kiss and tried to explain that I would not see her for a couple of days and next time she saw me she would have a new baby brother or sister. She just waved happily, blew me a big kiss and went off with her grandparents. This was the first time I had been separated from her since I had brought her home, and taking into consideration my hormones and the news I had just received with regard to her walking, I became quite emotional. It was probably a welcome release, because I think as humans we tend to bottle things up because sometimes to address things is much too complicated. It is easier to stay on what seems to be an even keel and carry on without letting in any extraordinary emotions or issues, so they do tend to stay buried and I think this is a survival mechanism. Being vulnerable just won't get the job done. However, on this day I suppose it was time for a release and I was unable to stay as controlled as I normally tried to be, and so I cried and I cried from my soul. It was almost cleansing and it was like someone had wiped off the writing from a white board and now it was ready to be written over again, and so I was ready to face the moment.

Once I had pulled myself together, which was some time later, I was put on a monitor and Martin and I went through our list of names for boys and girls, but remained firmly undecided on both. I had my various checks and then went out for dinner with friends to a local restaurant under the understanding that I were to be back in my room by 11 p.m., after which I was to eat or drink nothing until after the birth that was scheduled for eight the following morning.

A nurse woke me early the next day offering me a nice cup of tea. I told her that I was due to go down to have a baby and she said that it would be fine I was only having an epidural and not a general anaesthetic. I accepted gratefully only to find out that the nurse was an idiot and had made a mistake and consequently the whole thing had to be delayed until ten o' clock.

The operating theatre was a bit like a circus ring. Dr Millett and Martin were practising their golf swings, Mr Smith was telling jokes and I just lay there with my insides being cut open waiting to hear the sound of my child's cry.

She was born at 10.40 a.m. on Thursday 17th May 1990, weighing in at a whopping seven pounds and thirteen ounces. She had a mop of black curly hair and the loudest cry I had ever heard. All the sweet little gentle girls names that I had thought I might use were totally wrong for this child that was going to make her presence known to the world in not the quietest manner possible.

She was handed to me wrapped in a white fluffy towel and a new love enveloped me and I knew that there would always be room in my heart for more.

Sasha Rebecca came home a week later and Jodi loved her instantly; there was never a moment in Jodi's life when I thought that she may be feeling a touch of sibling rivalry. It was as if the only emotions that Jodi was capable of were loving and good ones. She cried if she were in pain or sad, but rarely became angry. If she ever became frustrated she was easily distracted, and she adored her new sister in a way I never believed possible.

It was almost as if history were repeating itself, because I don't ever remember feeling any jealousy to either of my sisters when they suddenly arrived home. I wonder if those emotions are perhaps genetic, or are they brought about by the environment in which we are raised, and that environment is passed down from one generation to the next and each time it is handed down it is with a slight variation, even though the main construction tends to stay the same.

CHAPTER 41

I t was a lovely summer that year, and we spent our days playing in the garden, going for walks in the park, feeding the ducks and playing on the swings. Sasha slept little and was permanently hungry, while Jodi on the other hand ate bird like quantities and was still capable of vomiting copious amounts at any given time of the day.

Part of our day's routine involved exercises set by the physio and occupational therapists in the hope that her development would be accelerated, but it was a slow process and required a lot of time and patience. The time was a little tricky, but I had endless amounts of patience and I would do whatever it took to ensure that my child would reach her full potential.

It was hard having two immobile babies. Everywhere I went I had to take the double buggy, and it was heavy and cumbersome, and often I couldn't get it down the aisles of certain shops. Occasionally I would become frustrated and give up and go home, but in the main I struggled in blissful oblivion.

Jodi by twenty months was beginning to stand unaided for a few seconds at the time, and then one day at the age of twenty-one months, contrary to professional opinion, she took her first steps. I became the mother of a toddler overnight, and the joy and elation was like no other. Once again she had defied the odds with pure determination and strength of character. She had begun to walk before her second birthday, and she was so proud of herself, and we were more than proud of her.

Meanwhile, Sasha was growing to be a beautiful, alert, bright baby and was already sitting up by the time she was four and a half months. She was climbing stairs and crawling at eight months, and was talking by a year. It was as if she had been sent to us to prove that there was somehow justice at a higher level. I had these two so very different children, both as determined to succeed as each other, but one quiet and passive and the other a little tornado who crawled like a bullet and climbed onto anything that she could access. And the most wonderful thing of all was that they absolutely adored each other. They were like twins, eating at the same times, sleeping together, and playing together. It wasn't long before Sasha became Jodi's interpreter.

There were often times that I was not able to understand what Jodi was trying to say and Sasha would soon tell me. Both understood everything that was being said to them and Sasha was very eloquent and made up for Jodi's inability to communicate, so she soon became her voice, and her crutch.

So life meandered along, and all was well. We moved again to a slightly bigger house in a slightly better location, and my girls were the light of my life. I missed them when I put them to bed at night and would delight at the mornings when I was greeted with outstretched arms and smiles of joy and expectations. We had a lovely little social life, making play dates with various friends, having lunches, teas and walks in the park. At least two or three times a week Jodi would have some kind of therapy, and Sasha would come along for the ride and would often join in not realising that she was not the intended victim.

I at this time had also started music classes for preschool children, and would hold five classes a week in my home. They were extremely popular and gave me some extra money, which came in very useful at the time. So life was full and fulfilled.

Jodi would have regular medical check ups with Dr Millett, and even though she was quite delayed in many of her skills and development, she was doing well, although Dr Millett always said that because of her problems at birth she may always be different and quite special.

One Sunday afternoon I took Jodi to a birthday party in a soft playroom. All her little friends were going and so were all their mothers. I had to leave Sasha at home with Martin, because she was not invited and she was really not happy about being left. When I arrived Jodi took off her shoes and went clambering onto the blown up plastic cushions of the soft play area. She looked so much tinier than all the other children and so unsteady I just wanted to go and pluck her out of the mass of children and take her home where she would be safe and out of view. It was when some of the mothers came up to me with that sympathetic look on their faces that meant that they felt very sorry for me and asked "How is Jodi now?" that in my mind it meant that she was so clearly different from everyone else, and they were asking me in a round about way how I was coping with the strain of a child that was not the norm.

We left straight after tea, before the hip hip hoorays, because that used to make her cry and then be sick as it was a loud noise, and I really didn't want to raise any more eyebrows than I needed to. By the time I arrived home I was distraught, and perhaps a little frustrated with myself because I had been living my life as though all was well and that everything would somehow resolve itself; that afternoon I realised that I had almost pulled the wool over my own eyes. I had convinced myself that everything would be alright and that in the end Jodi would be the same as every other child, and her development would catch up and in ten years time no one would ever know that there had ever been a problem. That afternoon I realised that things were not as I thought. As I watched my little girl struggling to stand in the soft play area, and unable to communicate with any of the other children it suddenly became clear that perhaps these last couple of years of blissful oblivion were sent to give me the strength to deal with what lay ahead. I walked into the house and burst out crying into Martin's arms, taking him completely by surprise, and I resolved to find out exactly what was wrong with my little girl.

So with the help of my health visitor and Dr Millett we took Jodi to a doctor at Watford General Hospital who, after a number of tests, called me in to tell me that Jodi had Mild Quadriplegic Cerebral Palsy. All the names she had used to label my child conjured up images of a child that didn't resemble Jodi in any way. I was actually speechless. I had often wondered how other people reacted when they are presented with a shock diagnosis, and I had always imagined scenes of extreme emotion, but it was not the case for me. I felt the bottom fall out of my stomach momentarily, and then I think I had the urge to laugh, because I suppose I didn't really believe what was being said to me, and then I found the familiar inner strength and need for control and I seemed to detach myself from my emotional soul and I proceeded to ask all the questions that I felt at this stage I needed the answers to. She couldn't tell me the full implications of her condition, but she categorically stated that she would need support in school and would need on-going therapy for the foreseeable future.

Looking back at pictures and videos all the signs were there, but hope and love is blind, and as Dr Millett subsequently said, we had nearly three years of enjoying our new life without worrying about Jodi's future or battling with authorities, and that time was the foundation to my strength and resolve to make sure that our daughter received all the help and support that she was entitled to.

Once again we were turning around another bend, but the road ahead was to be less smooth, and one with many hills and dales. Coming to terms with a child that had significant special needs was only the beginning of the next part of our journey. Martin and I had suddenly come to a crossroads, and without realising it we went in different directions.

Marriage is hard enough, but with the pressure of grief and dealing with a child that has special needs things become even tougher. Women tend to be far more accepting and have a more positive approach to life than men. Men find imperfection much harder to accept, and although Martin's love for Jodi didn't change, his attitude to her needs left a lot to be desired. It was as if he was in denial, and that for me was almost unacceptable, and so I threw myself into the role of mother and withdrew from the role of wife. Because Martin worked very long hours his input was minimal, and only took hold on a Saturday as Sundays he played golf, so we only had to endure him on a Saturday and that was enough to last a week. I also realised that I had a low tolerance for weakness and when Martin was around us he showed his weakness by becoming a bully. I think I allowed this behaviour because I didn't want to upset the equilibrium of my family, and if I confronted the situation I was afraid of what might happen. So life with my husband was not so rosy anymore, although it is only on reflection that I realise how bad it actually was, at the time it was my normal.

CHAPTER 42

Jodi started nursery school in the September before her third birthday. To get her toilet trained in preparation was so difficult I didn't think it would ever happen. I would cry to my mum, despairing of her inability to control her bladder, and she would promise me that she would be dry by the time she reached adulthood. I at the time doubted it. I had read books and information about children that were diagnosed with the same thing and bladder control was always marked as a difficult skill to learn.

On one occasion when in the Early Learning Centre with my friend Debbie, all the children were running around playing with all the display toys and every few minutes we would look down to see another puddle of wee collected in a little pool by Jodi's foot. Eventually after leaving at least five of these Debbie whispered that she thought that perhaps it was time to make a quick exit, as the puddles seemed to be attracting some attention from shop assistants and shoppers alike. Although we found the incident quite funny and have laughed about it since, it was for me another hurdle to jump, and it seemed to be such a high one.

However, true to form, one day Jodi just clicked and there was no looking back. No more accidents and off to nursery we went, and I can honestly say that I could rank that experience as probably one of the more challenging ones of that time. Although in saying that, most of Jodi's milestones were a challenge for her and for me, but the toilet training was harder for me than for her!

Apart from leaving Jodi with my mum, we had never been separated, and Jodi, whilst extremely friendly and affectionate when I was standing nearby, was not quite so happy when I tried to leave her with the staff at the nursery. It was in fact so traumatic for us both; it was as if someone was trying to cut off my arm. This child that I had given my life and soul to, who was so attached to me and me to her was now being expected to go off with strange women and leave me for a whole morning. I stood outside the door the first morning after she had been prised from my arms and I sobbed as hard as she did. Eventually they came to get me as they couldn't calm her down and they were a little concerned that her breathing was so fast and that she may need medical assistance. It turned out that I had to stay with her for a good three weeks to try and settle her and then I began leaving her for a few minutes at a time and built it up slowly. It was three months before I was able to leave her for the entire morning, by which time Sasha loved going to nursery so much I used to have to drag her out kicking and screaming to take her home, whilst Jodi was wrenched from my arms kicking and screaming (although she always settled after a few minutes).

So whilst Jodi played at nursery every morning, and Sasha slept every morning, I would make my endless calls to different areas of the local authorities, trying to get the necessary help in order to ensure my child an education that she deserved and was indeed her right.

The LEA (Local Education Authority) did everything in their power to plead that Jodi was not special needs enough to justify a "Statement of Educational Needs". This is a document that states what a child's needs are and how the local authority is prepared to implement the help that the child requires. The needs could range from anything from one hour of teaching support to twenty-three hours of classroom assistance, and often speech and occupational therapy is written into the statement to be provided in school by the local authority. The only problem is that each local authority works to a very tight budget and each child with a statement costs them more money.

We had been told by all of Jodi's doctors and therapists that if she were to go into school with no help we would be setting her up to fail. There was absolutely no way I was prepared to let that happen, I was not getting this far to then give up. So I fought. I wrote to MPs and heads of local authorities, I had Jodi assessed by private therapists to counteract the diagnosis of the reports made by the people allocated by the local authority, I called my key worker at the LEA every day and wrote to them every week. I threatened them with going to the press and vowed that Jodi would not be going to school until the appropriate help was put into place.

Every few weeks another letter would arrive saying that Jodi was not severe enough and therefore would not need any help and I would cry with anger and frustration. I couldn't understand why they would not help her. She was a child with potential and with the correct help in her early years may not need quite so much input in her adult life. Surely she was a good investment, and whilst I understood that severely disabled children needed more input, how could they justify not helping children like Jodi, who without it would not achieve at all, yet with the right input their worlds could be opened.

Martin would leave for work early in the morning and arrive home well after the children were in bed, and on the weekend he was irritable and frustrated. He would try to make Jodi do things that were beyond her capabilities and she would end up crying and hysterical and I ended up hating him. He would not accept that we had a child that was not the same as other children and so his time at home was strained and he began to spend as little time as possible with us. That suited me as I didn't have to deal with him and his issues on top of everything else. We did, however, have an extremely active life in the bedroom; Martin seemed to want sex almost every night, and I felt guilty if I refused him for some reason. Even till this day I have yet to work it out.

However, in the meantime Jodi was having very bad episodes of tonsillitis and it was decided that in the April, two months before Stephanie's wedding, that she would have to have them removed. Just before she was due to go into hospital we went to Leeds to visit my friends Debbie and David who had been relocated there on business. When we arrived I felt very queasy and a little out of sorts and expressed that had I not had a coil (a form of contraception that is 90 per cent safe) I would think that I were pregnant, but that couldn't be because I was practically infertile five years ago and this would be the other extreme. Debbie suggested we do a test anyway just as a laugh. It was not such a laugh when the result came out positive. I was absolutely stunned and quite shaken. I was certainly not planning on having another baby at the moment, not with Steph's wedding coming up, the strain of trying to get Jodi her statement, and also having to be in and out of hospital with her every few weeks. I was not sure I would be able to cope with being pregnant at that moment. Nevertheless, this was yet another sign from above and it is what was meant to be. If this is what was intended then I decided that it could only be a good thing and like everything else I would take it in my stride and it would be a wonderful blessing.

So the dress that I was planning for the wedding was changed and I went to a place in the back of beyond and chose one that I would hire for the day. Everyone after the shock waves had settled was delighted with my news of yet another arrival and Mr Smith was the most overwhelmed by the news; he said that after the baby was born I would be written up in medical history. However, the fact that I had fallen pregnant with a coil did carry its own risks and he suggested an early scan.

Jodi went into hospital in early April for her tonsillectomy and they said that she should only be there for two nights. I suspected that they were a little optimistic but kept my concerns to myself. The operation was anything but straight forward. She refused to eat and had to be drip fed, and her drip kept blocking, which meant that they had to keep changing it to different places. Her veins were so dreadful from her prematurity and all the blood tests and drips that she had had to endure during that time, that the whole thing became a nightmare and we were still in hospital after a week. During a quiet moment I decided that I may as well have a scan and make sure child number seven was doing what it was supposed to. So off I tootled to the ultrasound department. I was very familiar with the staff down there, and I was treated a little like royalty, which was quite lovely for me; after all it didn't happen very often. Once again the cold jelly was squirted onto my belly and the black and white images appeared on the screens. All seemed fine although the embryo did look quite small, but there was a heartbeat, and it was suggested that I return in a month to make sure that it had grown.

It is quite an amazing miracle that of conception and the most intriguing thing about it is the immediate attachment I felt to this tiny flicker of a speck. I often wondered if it was the idea of what it is going to be that I connected with or if it was actually the miniscule glimmer of life that found its way directly to my heart, but I knew that this baby was wanted and already loved as much as all the others that had gone before it.

Jodi eventually came out of hospital after ten days. Once again she went from being quite unwell and unable to eat or drink to suddenly turning the corner and becoming the happy lively toddler we were expecting her to be. So we finally went home and Sasha was delighted to have us there again, although she was becoming accustomed to spending nights with my parents every time Jodi was rushed into hospital for one thing or another, and I suppose she just accepted it as part of her life.

The day after we had arrived home I had a show of blood, and felt alarm bells going off in my head. I always felt for some reason that nothing else would happen, that I wouldn't lose any more babies because I had already lost so much, and if there was a greater power would it really be so uncompassionate?

Once again life was about to deal me yet another rotten hand. I went for another scan two weeks later, and it was discovered that the embryo had not developed any more since the first scan and there was no longer a heartbeat. I had lost the baby, and although I hadn't really planned this one and it was nothing like the losses that I had already encountered, I felt very sad, and almost cheated, and extremely angry. I felt that it was enough. How much more was I supposed to endure? What would be the straw that broke my back? And how many more times was I expected to bounce back? I felt as though I was being worn down, and my faith was diminishing, for with every blow I was becoming more confused as to how anyone could worship this entity that causes so much pain and suffering; how can anyone give thanks to that? I looked around not just at my own life and tried to work out if the good did actually outweigh the bad and I wasn't sure any more. I felt that I could no longer rely on this God of sorts to get me through my life; the only person that could help me was me.

I did get through it, and I did apparently look lovely at my sister's wedding, but another part of my heart had turned a little harder, and another chapter was locked away in a corner of my brain, perhaps to be dealt with at a later date.

I wanted Jodi to go to a Jewish primary school in Edgware, which was out of borough, and the headmaster there was happy to take her on the understanding that she had a full statement of educational needs, and that meant she was getting support for twenty-two hours a week. I knew that all her therapists would have to be seen outside school, because there was no way a therapist from one authority would travel to a school that was maintained by a different local authority, it would be much too complicated for the funding to be worked out, but that was fine as all I wanted was classroom support.

September 1993 was when Jodi was supposed to start school full time. She knew that all her friends from nursery were about to start, and every day she would ask me if we could go and get her uniform, but I had to say no, because as we still had no statement they were offering two hours a week, and it was totally unacceptable. So whilst all her friends went off to school and her younger sister went off to nursery, Jodi stayed home with me, and she never complained, but I knew she knew that she was different, and whilst she smiled and danced her days away I cried inside for what she was being denied.

I never gave up or backed down. I felt alone and alienated, yet my resolve never wavered, not for a second. I would get my child what she deserved because it was her right to have an education and one that she could access, and it was my job to ensure that it happened.

Then one day at the end of September the letter arrived. The local education authority had had a meeting and they had decided to offer Jodi a statement which stated that she would be given twenty-two hours a week welfare support, plus an hour of speech therapy, but I would have to take her to a clinic in Elstree as the therapist was not authorised to go out of borough.

My little girl was about to start school, we had won another fight, and as we stood in the uniform shop and the owner searched for a uniform small enough to fit this tiny little girl with enough determination and fight to put any man to shame, I looked on and sobbed.

In six years I had become someone else; a person driven by maternal instinct. It is something that should never be under estimated, and something to be used and embraced. I had stood up for something I believed in so strongly, and had laid the ground rules for the future. I knew that there would be plenty of fights ahead and that there were many things that I needed to address (my marriage being one of them), but I also knew that I had an inner strength that would drive me through every hurdle, and I would stand up for what I believed to be right from this day on.

CHAPTER 43

Jodi loved going to school. It was only a couple of weeks before she had cemented her relationship with her welfare support, Jeanette. She talked about her incessantly and approached all tasks set by Jeanette with immense enthusiasm. She was forming friendships with her peer group some of which would continue to this day.

Sasha had started kindergarten and went every morning until 12.15, so I had the mornings alone. Something that only five years earlier I was accustomed to, but now although it was welcome it was not really what I would have chosen. I spent my mornings keeping busy cleaning my house or cooking and shopping, but everything that I did was for the good of my children, they were my purpose, and my drive.

However, since my earlier miscarriage I felt that I was somehow incomplete and that some of the grief and devastation from the previous five years had somehow been released into a disorderly mess in my head. Some of the emotions that I did not have the strength to deal with at the time had seemed to be triggered during the loss of my most recent failed pregnancy, and I suppose having to deal with yet another setback had unbalanced the equilibrium of my coping mechanism a little. I decided that I needed to talk to someone to help me to rearrange the mess in my head and put it all back into neat little piles of grief that I could somehow cope with and therefore lead a normal controlled life.

I started to see a counsellor every week for an hour, and she asked me all the right questions. I told her the tragic story of my four beautiful baby boys and I cried and lay blame on people that I had not really thought to blame in the past. I suppose the hardest loss for me to come to terms with was Benjamin, because I had always felt as though the doctors interfered with his machines on that last day, and if they had left him alone then maybe he would have become stronger and more resilient and in a few more weeks he may have shown improvement; I realised that I felt cheated and robbed of my son. The other boys were so sick that there was nothing that anyone could have done to save them, so during those counselling sessions I lay to rest some ghosts, and yet realised some truths about myself including the guilt that I felt. I always somehow believed that it was my fault that the quins had to be delivered so early. I felt as though when at twenty-six weeks they had told me that they were viable I had given up, because it was almost to the day that the pre-eclampsia had started, and so I had carried this guilt with me without knowing how to express it. Although I still do feel that I was responsible in some way for their prematurity I somehow have learnt to live with this knowledge, but until this day, Jodi is a constant reminder of my weakness and it explains my resolve to never show my vulnerability nor give in to challenges too great again. I learnt to understand my need for control and my determination to succeed. I spent many sessions crying, but on one occasion the counsellor was so upset with my tale that I ended up comforting her. I don't think that was part of her intended therapy, and I actually found it quite amusing!

On my last visit to her it was as if a cloud had lifted and I could suddenly see clearly, but it was almost more than that. Just as four years ago when I was standing by the grave of my sons and the sun lit up the stone and I realised that I was pregnant, on this day I had the same feeling. As I stood in the office of this woman who had opened my mind and heart over the last few weeks I knew beyond all doubt that I was pregnant, and I knew also that this time it would be okay and in nine months I would give birth to a healthy baby. I felt as though I now had guardian angels. My sons determined from high in the heavens my destiny and I just had to help them along the way. Once again I had put my pain and grief away into the corners of my mind and each little pile had a "dealt with" sticker attached.

Martin greeted the news of my pregnancy with moderate enthusiasm, but he was much more concerned at the time with making as much money as possible and socialising with all his funny people from the golf club, or from work. Every so often another person would appear and we would have to see them for dinner and become friends with them until they no longer had a purpose and then we wouldn't see them anymore.

I, however, still had the same friends and occasionally would meet someone new that I would click with and those people still remain in my life today. Mum and dad now lived locally and Stephanie was married and so living the life of "Sadie married lady", and although my marriage was quite lonely the rest of my life was at the time full and fulfilled.

We had some time previously moved into yet another house on Martin's insistence and it was in dire need of decoration. Martin decided to do these works toward the end of my pregnancy when I was at my most cumbersome and exhausted, but for some reason I just let him take over and all I did was choose the colours.

Jodi was still having quite a large amount of therapy and I would often have to pick her up from school and take her to different therapists and then drop her back. Sasha had had enough of being the only child in her class to come home at lunch time whilst all the others were there until three o'clock, and as much as it broke my heart to be without her all day, she had exerted her right as a little person and I had to listen to her. So during the long days on my own I would eat copious amounts of chocolate and sweets whilst cleaning and ironing and doing all the chores that Martin had given me in the morning before he left for work, and all around me there were builders and their mess.

Stephanie announced her pregnancy soon after the New Year, which would mean that there would be about ten weeks between her baby and mine. It was as if our childhood games were coming true. All those years ago we used to dream of these times and now miraculously they seemed to be happening.

My baby was due in June and once again Mr Smith insisted on a caesarean, and so we assembled the usual team of anaesthetists, nurses and Mr Millet the paediatrician, and once again chose a date that would suit everyone.

So on 22nd June 1994 I went to the Portland Hospital once again, leaving my house in unfinished chaos, with Martin's promise to have it cleaned and ready for me on my return. I had my usual checks and once again went with friends to have a light snack to return before ten after which I was not able to eat or drink again until after the birth. The next morning when they woke me I was sure not to be tempted by any offers of tea, and so at 8.30 prompt I was taken down to theatre where an hour later our third beautiful daughter was born. Emma Natalie, born at 9.40 a.m. on 23rd June 1994, was delivered at seven pounds and one ounce, and she was the most beautiful newborn I think that I had ever seen. I fell in love instantly with her and knew beyond all doubt that I would enjoy every second of this child.

Jodi and Sasha came later in the day to see Emma with my parents and both children were in awe of her size and her inability to do anything, and whilst they were even more excited with the gifts that baby Emma had apparently bought for them, I knew also that they had also fallen in love with this tiny bundle.

Five days later on a balmy summer's day I took my new baby home, and once again thoughts of what might have been flickered through my mind and I felt the usual sadness and uncontrollable grief, but I held my baby girl and closed my eyes to recover from the moment and found my strength in her and my waiting children who filled my life and heart with every moment of their existence.

CHAPTER 44

Once again life took on a routine. I relished my role as mother. My days were filled with my children and I enjoyed my time with Emma when the others were at school. When Emma was ten weeks, on 31st August 1994, I was standing in my lounge ironing, it was ten o' clock at night and the phone rang. It was Nicholas my brother-in-law calling to tell me that Stephanie had given birth to a baby boy. He was healthy and well and both mum and baby were fine. I was not expecting my reaction. I was so delighted for them and yet I cried so hard. I would like to say that I cried tears of joy and I am sure some of them were, but I think I cried tears of grief. I would never begrudge my sister nor for that matter anyone anything, but in that moment I actually felt sorry for myself, a self indulgent emotion that I had always tried so hard to suppress, and here I was on the happiest moment of my sister's life crying for myself again and for what might have been. It was the strangest feeling; I felt that I desperately needed to be with her, and that I needed to take control of her and her new baby so that I could ensure that nothing bad would happen to either of them. I suppose I felt that if I was totally involved with her life that it would somehow help to heal the wound that had once again opened after so many months of being closed, and that as a result I would once again be able to control my grief.

The summer passed and in the September Sasha started Primary school. So both my older children were in the same place, and I think Sasha knew instinctively that she would have to be Jodi's protector in school. So whilst Jodi believed that she was showing her younger sister the ropes of big school, in actual fact Sasha was weighing up the role that she would have to play and how much Jodi would need her to be her guardian.

In hindsight I don't know if perhaps I had made a mistake in sending them both to the same school. I am not sure that the responsibility was too great for a four-year-old, or whether it was just how it is with a sibling that has learning difficulties. I know that Sasha was always older than her years and almost became another mother not only to Jodi but also to Emma. She took on the role as my assistant from the start, and once they started school together this position developed and has continued to do so ever since. When speaking to Sasha now she remembers that she was different from other children in that she felt that she had more responsibility, although she felt it more in their later school years, and perhaps she was not so aware of the significance in her earlier years. She never felt that she was the second oldest in the family, she has always taken on the role of older sister, and conveys now that growing up with a child like Jodi has made her into a very different person to the child that she probably would have been had she been born into a family that did not have the same difficulties.

During these years Jodi appeared to be on the same level as her peer groups socially and so she was happy and settled and in turn so was the whole family. I don't remember anything apart from being a wife and mother during that time. It was as if I was almost a non-person. As much as I loved being a mother and put my life and soul into it, and I would not swap that role for the world, I think as a person I somehow became lost. I do feel though the same could be said for any woman with very young children. Our days are filled with nappies and shopping and bedtime stories and when everyone is finally asleep and settled for the night there is still the washing and cleaning and preparing for the following day, so by the time that precious moment comes when you can just sit and do nothing you are almost incapable of even having an independent thought let alone an independent action. Then of course there is the husband that needs servicing and it is much easier to be subservient in that department, as it only takes a few minutes whereas an argument into why you are not in the mood could take hours!

To compensate for the lack of identity I think I consciously resolved to be the best mother that I possibly could. I very rarely shouted at my children and I spent hours playing and reading and stimulating their minds and souls. We would go for picnics in the park, have art and craft afternoons and music and dancing on other days. I would encourage them to play in the garden whatever the weather and would sit and teach them to read and write whenever I could. My life was devoted to making them the best that they could possibly be, and I was so proud of the people that they were becoming. I had read once that 90 per cent of what a parent says to their child is instruction and that they very rarely have conversations about anything else; well I was determined that 90 per cent of our conversations would not be commands or direction, but just conversation. So our home was filled with cheerful chatter and extremely happy children.

That time passed with almost uneventful routine. I still believed that Jodi's main problems were motor related, in that she would just have more physical problems than the average person, but that sooner or later she would be able to compensate for them with different strategies. I continued to take her to different therapists, and I started to search for alternative therapists and programmes that would help her develop further and faster. I would never accept that there may have been a ceiling to Jodi's potential, so I persevered and if one therapist had exhausted all her resources then we moved on to the next.

When Emma was a year old we moved house yet again. This time we moved to a tiny house on a huge plot of land. It was Martin's intention to sell some of the land or build a house on it, but the planners would not allow that so we decided to build the house for ourselves. So six months after we moved into the house the builders moved in too. Once again I took it all in my stride and carried on as if there really wasn't chaos and bedlam all around me.

One day I was having tea at my friend Michelle's and felt a little queasy and not quite myself. I then did a quick calculation in my head and realised that my period was late. Oh dear, this was probably not ideal as Martin had made it quite clear that he really did not want any more children, even though I wanted at least another three. Martin tended to always get his own way on everything. Michelle convinced me to buy a test on the way home. I desperately wanted it to be positive. I remember thinking that it was really bizarre that waiting for the test results could conjure up the exact same stirrings as all those many moons ago when I was almost guaranteed a negative result. I guess some emotions will remain no matter what, I think it is a little like Pavlov's dogs; the association causes the reaction. Needless to say, however, the test was in fact positive. I had to call Michelle before Martin as I needed advice on how best to break the news to him. After all, our house was being demolished and apparently rebuilt around us, I had three young children, one of which needed constant attention and probably would for the foreseeable future, and more importantly the cost of another child for Martin would be the thing that he would be most worried about. Oh, happy days! I would just have to tell him straight out. I did and his reaction thankfully was not as bad as I thought it was going to be, although he did say that he did not want any involvement with this child and that as compensation he should be allowed to play golf whenever he wanted. I agreed. It suited me, I was getting another baby and he was staying out of the way more. Fantastic!

I lost the baby at nine weeks; it was the same as last time. I felt that once again Martin had his own way, and once again I cried my silent tears. He didn't even pick me up from the hospital after the procedure, he sent my friend Stacey. I didn't think anything of it. That was my life.

CHAPTER 45

Snow had settled like a thick blanket of white cotton on the ground and as I gave the children breakfast they watched through the window as the builders negotiated their way through the snow and up the path. Sasha commented nonchalantly whilst munching on her coco pops that one of the builders had fallen over and had not yet emerged. I was too busy trying to feed everyone and ignored her. The builder had broken his arm. The team were now one man down. This house was taking forever and it seemed that it would never be completed. I was trying to remain calm and optimistic and pretend that we were not really living in hellish circumstances, but it did sometimes get to me, and I was finding it increasingly difficult to behave like a normal rational person. Martin left the house early in the morning before the children woke and returned after they had gone to sleep so did not see the difficulties that we were enduring, and I rarely complained. Until one day, we returned home and I could smell the unmistakeable odour of gas permeating around the house and knew for absolute certainty that to stay in this house any longer was an impossibility. So I called my parents without even asking permission from my husband and we moved into their house immediately.

It was such a relief to be in a home where there was not a thick layer of dust covering every surface, and to sleep soundly and not worry that the children were being affected by the environment that we were expecting them to live in.

It was a cold hard winter that year, and living with my parents, although a million times better than living in our house, was not easy. Martin needed my attention when he returned late in the evening and I was torn between him and my mum and dad. Although my mum always told me that my husband should always be my priority, even over my children (which I strongly disagree with) I still found that I would rather eat all together earlier in the evening and not have to wait until nine or ten at night when Martin would eventually return home.

Stephanie was already pregnant with her second baby who was due in the April of that year and I was feeling the loss of the baby that I should have been carrying and no longer was. It was still a bone of contention with Martin and me, and he still insisted that he really did not want another baby and that if we did by any chance decide to have one then it would be more or less my responsibility and I was not to expect him to help at all. This actually was fine as he really didn't do that much for any of them and I was happy with that arrangement. It meant that I could raise them the way that I thought fit, and I didn't have to battle against his upbringing. Having said that, on the weekend he did try to exert his discipline and this often made for quite unpleasant scenes and I would dread the weekends for fear of what they may bring.

In the February temperatures dropped and both Jodi and Sasha became quite ill. Sasha had an ear infection and Jodi had started coughing, and I knew the implications as they still remained the same. I sat in the doctor's surgery, and with Sasha quietly moaning in pain, and Jodi unable to stop coughing, we looked such a sorry sight that one of the patients that was in the queue before us gave up her turn so that we could take it. The doctor gave Sasha antibiotics and gave Jodi a letter to have her admitted into hospital. My mum had the same virus so Stephanie was left looking after my two younger children and I took Jodi to the Portland Hospital again.

After many tests and nebulisers I realised that I had to feed the meter of my car, so I left Jodi in the hospital and as soon as I was outside I lit up a cigarette and then ran to the car, fed the meter, lit up another cigarette and ran back to the hospital where I went straight to the pharmacy to fill a prescription so that we could take Jodi home as Martin didn't want her in overnight (against the advice of everyone). I handed the prescription over to the pharmacist and suddenly the room started spinning. I couldn't speak and I started to feel myself slipping out of consciousness and I fainted there in the pharmacy department of the Portland Hospital. I eventually came round and pulled myself together and a nurse from Jodi's ward was sent to come and collect me. Martin was called but said that he couldn't get there until much later in the day and I soon felt considerably better. One of the nurses whom I had known from six years ago suggested that I may be pregnant again and I decided that I would think about that option when I knew that Jodi was on the road to recovery, which at that moment was not the case.

Martin came to collect us later that evening. He left his car at his office and drove mine home, and asked in passing if I was feeling better. As I suspected Jodi deteriorated during the night and in the very early hours of the morning we had to return to hospital, where we remained for a further three days. By the time I returned home, Sasha was well again and so was mum so things became somewhat normal.

A week later my period still had not arrived and I didn't really need a test to confirm my suspicions because this time I knew all the signs only too well. I summoned up the courage and after serving Martin with his dinner and talking about every other subject conceivable, I gently broke the news that another child was growing inside me and that this time it was in fact down to his sloppy withdrawal methods and nothing to do with me. He was more annoyed that I hadn't told him straight away, but seemed quite happy with the idea of another baby especially as it meant golf whenever he wanted. His life in theory would not change an awful lot. I could not have been happier, but this time I felt much more cautious. I was not above tragedy. Bad things, I had learnt, happened to people over and over again and it really didn't matter how good as a person you were, it still didn't make any difference. I would actually say the better a person you were the more likely it was that terrible things would happen, so I felt very nervous about this pregnancy and told Martin that I insisted that he should be at all my scans for this baby, I couldn't face awful news alone anymore. He begrudgingly agreed.

I called Mr Smith and told him that I was expecting yet another baby and he was delighted for me as always, and suggested an early scan, but this time I refused. I just wanted to enjoy being pregnant for a while longer than last time and decided that I would be the same as all other mothers and not have my first scan until thirteen weeks. Also I had to consider that my life was so busy at the moment, what with the house that needed constant supervision and Martin constantly sending me on errands to look for all the accessories that it needed: bathrooms, kitchens, floors, tiles, etc. Thank goodness for my father, because I had such terrible morning sickness with this baby that being on the go all day was quite draining. But he took me wherever I needed to go and was patient and sensitive to all my needs, and to make matters just a little more challenging I had to do everything with a toddler in tow. I also had the various therapists and programmes that I had to take Jodi to during the day and after school, and then I had to make sure that she was achieving all the goals that had been set for her and that meant a programme at home that had to be carried out every day. So if I didn't have to go to town for an extra scan, even if it meant that I only had to give up a day, it was better for me.

Stephanie gave birth to another baby boy on 24th April at one in the morning. I had my head down the toilet when mum received the news and came running in to tell me (my morning sickness wasn't limited to the morning). I didn't react the same way this time, because now we lived in the same road as each other and our lives had become completely intertwined, I knew that like his big brother Jack, this new baby would be the next best thing to a son of my own. Plus I had much too much to think about and didn't really have the energy to get emotional in the same way as I had when Jack was born.

I had my first scan just after Sam's circumcision. I decided not to take my car as I thought that if the worst happened and it was not good news I would not be able to drive back. I knew that this was my last chance for another baby; Martin had made that perfectly clear. That train journey was the longest and the hardest one I had ever made. Every scenario ran through my head and I tried to rationalise with myself that I already had what I thought I never would and that I was so much luckier than so many other people in this world. Not only that, Jodi was a walking miracle and I told myself that I should be grateful that she was here and that my other children too were the most precious gifts and if the worst did happen again I could take comfort in them. It didn't help! I wanted this baby, it didn't matter about anything else, this baby was part of me now; it was part of my future either way. The thought of losing this one was unbearable; I didn't think I would have the strength to ever come to terms with another loss. Someone must have been looking down on me that day and I suspect it was my sons. The scan was fine, I was carrying a healthy baby and there was no reason to worry anymore. Of course I worried until the day of the birth.

Eventually we moved back into our house and although the builders were still living there with us it was paradise in comparison to what it had been.

On 31ˢᵗ October at 9.45 in the morning, Tamara Beth was born weighing in at seven pounds seven ounces. She seemed like a clone of Emma so much so that I spent the first week calling her Emma. I brought her home after three days. She was my hardest delivery and longest recovery. Martin insisted that I should be sterilised at the time of the caesarean. This was my last baby. I could never again be pregnant. Another little part of my heart was broken.

CHAPTER 46

Life with four children was idyllic and because of the age gap it was almost as if I had two separate families. Jodi and Sasha went off to school every day and Emma started a couple of mornings at nursery, so I spent all my days with my children and of course my sister Stephanie.

Tamara spent a large part of her day wearing her coat, what with all the therapists and school runs that I had to do each week, but she didn't really seem to mind. Unfortunately, however, she had recurring ear infections resulting in me spending a large amount of time in the doctor's surgery with her.

Martin was true to his word and really didn't have very much to do with her; I don't actually think she realised that she had a father. I actually loved this part of my life. Although my marriage was not perhaps the best it really didn't matter because I was fulfilled in other ways. I still believe that it is not possible to be totally satisfied with every part of your life, because then what would you aspire to and without aspirations wouldn't life become dull?

A large amount of my energies at that time were invested in trying to find a programme that would help Jodi reach her full potential. School life was becoming increasingly more challenging for her and her social skills were not advancing at the same rate as everyone else. Whereas up until that point she had always been quite a sociable little thing, she seemed to be becoming more and more insular, and at home the activities that she chose were ones that didn't need any interaction. She was also extremely obsessive, so when one day it was announced that there had been a severe case of dysentery in schools in the area and all children were advised to wash their hands extremely well with soap regularly and especially after using the toilet, Jodi took every instruction on board and two weeks later her hands were red raw, dry and peeling. We had to somehow break her obsession, but it was no easy feat. She would also spend hours watching television and was fixated with Superman. So much so that one day she declared that she thought that she actually had powers and that she knew that if she had to, she could fly. We knew then that she may need extra supervision!

I was determined to treat her no differently from any of my other children and in the same way I was determined that my other children didn't feel that I put more energy into Jodi because of her needs. So I ensured that I devoted the same amount of time to each child, and that whatever their talent I encouraged them to pursue it. As time moved on I spent more and more time ferrying and dropping off at different activities.

When Jodi was ten she was being badly bullied at her school. Sometimes I don't think she even knew what was happening, but when she was physically pushed and scratched she knew that what was happening was wrong, and after a while she seemed not to smile as much and her light seemed to diminish. I cried so many tears in those times. I couldn't bear that after all this child had endured and accomplished something like bullying was breaking her spirit. Not only that, it was breaking mine, because I couldn't bear to see her suffer anymore and I was unable to make the school see it for what it was. The worst thing was that if they were unable to control it with a child that had welfare support, what was happening to other children who were not as guarded, but just as weak, or different in another way? I cried the tears of a mother for her daughter. Those were the tears that are shed when your child is hurting and there is nothing that you can do to help, and I cried tears of frustration and anger because I couldn't get through to the teachers involved that what was happening was unacceptable. I tried my very best to think of my glass as half full, but when a child is suffering there is no upside. Eventually I made the decision to move her school, and at the same time we had to move Sasha as well. She didn't mind, it was all a bit of an adventure and it meant that she could be with her best friend Victoria. Jodi settled in well initially but it soon became apparent that even with no bullying she was struggling with normal life and integration. I wouldn't let it bring me down, I just became more determined to find a way to make things right for her.

Tamara was growing into a gorgeous toddler who was completely attached to me. She adored me and followed me wherever I went. She would stand behind my legs peeking shyly out at anyone that spoke to her. The only person that I could leave her with was Stephanie and even then it was for very short periods of time. She was the typical youngest child, and was treated that way by the whole family. I loved her adoration and I adored her more than she could ever return, but I felt the same for each one of my precious little girls. They were my life and my life force. They were the reason that I was who I was and that I had the drive and motivation to achieve the things that I did. There was no other part of my life at that time they were it.

Emma started school the year that Jodi transferred to secondary school and Tamara went to nursery, which was quite traumatic as it meant she had to leave me for a few hours every day. I suddenly had my mornings to myself again and I wasn't quite sure what to do with them. I joined a gym and gasped my way around some of the machines all the time thinking that fitness was just not for me. As soon as I had left the building I would light up a cigarette and buy myself some sort of unhealthy snack, usually a cream egg or a bar of galaxy! But it was fun meeting up with friends and having a gossip over a cup of tea after a workout, or even just the gossip and the tea and not bothering with the workout! On the mornings that I couldn't summon up the energy to go to the gym, which was why more often than not, I visited my parents, or sister, and occasionally a friend. Sometimes I even ventured off to go shopping, but this was really not my favourite pastime. I toyed with the idea of a job, but quickly dismissed that thought; I still had to take Jodi off to various therapists during the day so I really couldn't possibly have a job commitment. Still, the mornings passed quickly and it was not long before Tamara was home.

When a Jewish girl reaches the age of twelve it is customary to have a ceremony. For a boy it is thirteen and called a bar mitzvah and for a girl a bat mitzvah. It is a ceremony that signifies the passing of childhood and the onset of adulthood. We were making Jodi's in November 2000. The girls usually make a presentation of some sort relaying a story from the Old Testament and relating it to their own life. Jodi spoke about when Sarah became pregnant at the age of one hundred after being barren. It was quite poignant, and her presentation was exceptional. All our guests were not only astounded with her confident and eloquent performance, but choked at her personal achievement, and when looking around there were many tears shed that day. For me, although emotional, it was one of the highlights of her life to that point, and my eyes were dry because I could only celebrate her and the joy that she had brought into our lives up until then.

It was a party that was like no other. I had never seen a room full of so many people so emotionally charged and each one delighting in this young lady who had climbed so many mountains to get to this point. When I reflected that day to the same time twelve years before, did I ever think for one minute that this day would have been possible? And I suppose the answer is yes, because I would never give in to any negativity and so the day would eventually have had to come as it would for all my girls in turn.

The next day brought a major change to our life yet again. Martin's boss fired him.

CHAPTER 47

When you lose a child it puts the rest of your life into perspective, and so when I realised the enormity of what had happened to Martin the day after the bat mitzvah, I approached it with calm and optimism. Nothing could be as horrific as outliving ones child so I knew for absolute certainty that I would survive this next drama.

I had never really trusted the boss and was always very wary of his intentions. I felt that he was very spoilt, and because of the money that he was worth I felt that he thought that it was his right to play with and wreck people's lives.

He was very quick to forget the out of duty calls that he had demanded from Martin, like sitting with the body of his dead father, or teaching his son his bar mitzvah, or listening to his wife's filthy jokes. As I recall none of these were written into Martin's contract.

A couple of weeks later on a Friday evening as we were sitting down to our chopped liver, egg and onions, recalling the festivities that had passed and discussing the future now that Martin was a free agent, there was a knock on the door. Outside stood a man in a suit brandishing two brown A4 envelopes, he asked for Martin and me by name then handed us the envelopes and walked hurriedly away.

The boss man had served us papers. He was suing us for breach of contract. I don't know why he was suing me, I didn't have a contract with him the stupid man. I wondered if he had not noticed that I didn't actually go to work or earn any money of my own, so what he was suing me for was beyond me.

Well this was another test that I was certainly not expecting. I had thought that just having Martin unemployed was quite a test on its own, even though I had no doubt that he would make money with or without a boss man. Now there was another component to deal with: we had to instruct solicitors and I had to engage my brain in order that I could work out what the hell was going on and what I was expected to do. I also had to know all the possible outcomes so that I could mentally prepare myself and come to terms with whatever I needed to face. I suppose I had learnt this coping strategy when the babies were ill. If I knew the worst then I could prepare myself for that, but aim for the best. That way I was never faced with shocked disappointment and was always delighted with anything better than the worst. I would not let the boss man get the better of me. He was a bully and he thought that by intimidating us he would make us unhappy, and would somehow make our lives miserable, but I would not let him break me, and although my children were perfectly aware that life had taken a different avenue, they never for one minute knew my stresses.

Martin on the other hand seemed to have really lost the plot. It reminded me of the day that Greg died when he could not focus and spoke incoherently and almost put a wall around himself so that the only person that was in his world was himself. I would say sometimes in our private moments that I was worried and that I wasn't sure what the outcome was going to be, and that I didn't know how I was involved when all I had been doing these past years was raising our children, and he would always, always reply, "Well how do you think I feel?" But I didn't care how he felt, he had somehow dragged us and especially me into this mess and it should have been his job to make it better, but he wasn't capable and I had to almost take over. I eventually told the solicitors to deal with me and not him as he couldn't take any more on board and was not making any sense.

I think that Martin had a breakdown and all those times in the past when he behaved in the same irrational way in times of extreme stress, I think that then too he had had some kind of breakdown. So suddenly I was not only mother to my children, but I had almost become carer to my husband, and all the respect that I had had for him, even though he was controlling and selfish in the past, had now completely diminished. It was as though his bravado of being so powerful was a complete farce. I now had to take the driving seat and look after my home, my children, and I was also faced with trying to sort out our future. I didn't want to feel that this time I may fail to hold it all together, but I was struggling to maintain an equilibrium. I couldn't sleep and often woke at five in the morning and took the dogs for a walk. I rarely sat and relaxed and the only way I was able to cope was to what I can only describe as put down my shutters. It was a strategy that I had used often in the past where I would almost consciously shut down my emotions so that I felt nothing, no pain no happiness, and no stress, nothing. I almost became a robot. It was the only way that I could cope with what lay ahead. Obviously, I did feel something which was why I was unable to sleep or eat, and smoked like a trooper, but that was all subconscious. I did also resort to alcohol in the evenings, and occasionally my evenings started quite early.

I took on a morning job at the local kindergarten working with two-year-olds. It nearly killed me. I had never been so exhausted, and poor Tamara who was also still only at nursery herself had to put up with a very tired mummy most afternoons. But she was the perfect child and as long as she could see me she was happy to play and occupy herself.

Martin and I spent many hours talking to solicitors and spending hours in their offices, often leaving the children with Stephanie or willing friends. I felt terribly guilty that suddenly I could not be there for them all the time and that for the first time there was an intrusion in our lives, something that was taking my energies away from my girls, the most important people in my life. I hated the boss man for that, and in my head I thought of him as no better than Hitler himself. At the same time I was beginning to hate Martin, because he was unable to be my rock, he was no longer a reliable source of comfort and I blamed him totally for the mess that we were now in. I had to almost become a different person in order to deal with him. I had to think of him as another child because otherwise I would have killed him!

Thankfully, in the February Martin made some money which meant that we could live for at least a year and that we would not have to sell our house at that moment. It also meant that we could join my parents in Florida for the Passover in the April. Martin decided that he would like to look at the possibility of emigrating to America. I think he was trying to avoid a possible court case, and I stupidly went along with the idea, although for a while it did seem quite appealing to start all over again somewhere else. In reality there is absolutely no way that I could have left my only support system and move away with five children, Martin being one of them.

We did come home from Florida and put the idea of running away behind us. Shortly after our return the court case was settled and it cost us dearly, and the money was the least of our costs. Once again a little part of me had changed and I had become stronger and more in control of my own life, even if it was not the perfect life, and at the same time another part of my soul had turned to stone and died. I felt almost that although my journey was teaching me so many lessons, I couldn't imagine that any good could come of them. It was not my place to question why, but I often wondered in those days the point that was being made. Would I have been so different if my journey had taken me on a completely different path? Am I really a better person as a result of what has happened to me? I wonder now if each challenge faced has helped me to cope and understand future challenges and perhaps my understanding of the world has altered. Whatever the reasons (if in fact there are any) I had come through yet another episode and I somehow managed to smile and laugh with my children. My love for them had only increased and they were still my life and my purpose. As for the rest of my life, well that remained challenging.

CHAPTER 48

In the June of that year we made Sasha her bat mitzvah. It was completely different from Jodi's, it didn't have the same emotional impact, instead it was very much a party and celebration of our daughter's life so far. Sasha was a truly exceptional person; she had a maturity and integrity that was rare to find in a child so young. She was funny and bright, yet so dizzy all at the same time. She was and still is wonderful company and so passionate about her beliefs whatever they might be. Celebrating her progression into adulthood seemed long overdue as she seemed to have been an adult for as long as I could remember.

It was a wonderful party and it felt so liberating knowing that we no longer had to worry about the boss man or any boss for that matter. I also felt that I needed to address the person that I was becoming. It was not the same person that had walked down the aisle eighteen years earlier, and although I was aware that there had been a significant change, I was unable to comprehend what that change was, and also how it would manifest itself.

During all the celebrations and self-searching, however, Jodi's future was also being mapped along different lines to those that I had expected. It was becoming more and more apparent that her social skills were completely stagnant. Although she was nearly fourteen years old, she was still behaving the same way as she had since she was ten. She really had no social life, the friends that she had at school were lovely to her and looked out for her, but they were to her how they were to Emma and Tamara. Jodi was out of her depth when they were talking about their current lives, about the boys that they fancied, or about the books that they had read or films that they watched. She was still talking about Superman and Spiderman and shooting imaginary people in the dark. Her life was becoming more and more insular, and I had to start thinking about where her future would be. I knew categorically that she would never be able to stay in a mainstream society, but I certainly didn't think she was severe enough to be institutionalised. I expressed my concerns to Dr Millett, and he was confident that either the Jewish community would provide something for people like Jodi, or that if all else failed that somehow I would ensure that a place was created that would cater for her needs. I thought that the former was much more likely.

I spoke to her school on several occasions and they were insistent that Jodi was doing so well and that her needs were not as bad as I was claiming. The thing with very orthodox Jews is that they tend to sweep things under the carpet. The school that Jodi was attending believed that they could handle all her needs, and whilst they did a remarkable job they too had limitations. Jodi had not developed socially, but they would not accept that, and that was fine because there really was no alternative place for her at that time. I did look at several options, but none were appropriate.

So life with Jodi continued to be challenging. She spent quite a substantial amount of time going to outside organisations that would help her with her difficulties and I spent a considerable amount of time taking her backwards and forwards from these places. However, since Martin was now working for himself he actually volunteered his chauffeuring services when he was available which did help me out. I stopped working for the kindergarten in the summer and went to work with Martin helping to build up the property management side. It was one of the biggest mistakes I had ever made. Our relationship was already having serious problems and we seemed to be arguing constantly about anything and everything. I think it was more me than him this time because once the crisis with the boss man had passed Martin had resumed his normal behaviour patterns, but I couldn't resume mine. There had been too much water under the bridge. I had had to be strong for everyone and I could not go back to being controlled and dictated to. So working together was not one of the best ideas that we had ever had.

In the summer of 2002 we went to Spain with Stephanie and Nicholas. We hired apartments next door to each other. It was a lovely holiday, except for the fact that Martin spent the majority of it having meetings with random people about buying flats, and if he wasn't thinking about property he was flirting with the group of divorced women that were also staying in the same complex as us.

It only became a problem for me when he left the children upstairs in the apartment alone so that he could sit and finish playing cards and making innuendos at the other women.

Jodi also started her periods on that holiday and insisted on announcing to the world why she was not allowed to go swimming. It also took me quite a while to make her understand how to look after herself in this new situation and I found that I would have to tend to her in the bathroom more often than not. As a mother it is something you don't expect to have to do for your child. When you say goodbye to the days of nappies you expect that the days of toilet training are over. Unfortunately, that was not the case for me, and I am sure that there are plenty of women with daughters in the same position as Jodi who have had to do the same duties. I tried not to give it much thought and resolved once again that this situation would not be permanent; Jodi would eventually be able to deal with this alone, and she does.

One afternoon as Stephanie and I were putting the world to rights whilst eating copious amounts of food, mainly French bread with cream cheese and jam, we decided that it would be a really good idea if, when we returned home after our holiday, we were to start training and become really fit. I had given up the cigarettes three months earlier and my body was showing the signs of over eating and lack of exercise. Plus I felt that a personal challenge would take my mind off the fact that my marriage was not so wonderful and it would give me a completely different focus and channel for my energies. It would be a positive step also in keeping me away from the nicotine sticks and would make me think more about the good that I could do for myself.

It was quite a novel idea in that I had never put an awful lot of effort into myself. I knew I scrubbed up well if we were going anywhere special, but as a general rule I looked a little tramp like during the days when I was cooking and cleaning and looking after my brood. I didn't really rate very highly in the scheme of things. So the thought of perhaps doing something that would ensure a healthier lifestyle, whilst at the same time make me look and feel better about me, was extremely appealing. We also decided that on our return we were going to have all our hair cut short.

I think that that was a real turning point in my life. I had decided that there was no room for negative energy. I had to make good of a not so good situation, and for the first time I was not going to be as selfless as I had been; I was actually going to do something that only I would benefit from. Of course in the long run so would the rest of the family in that I would have more energy and be fitter and healthier, but initially the reason that I had decided on this course of action was for me and me alone.

So on my return to England I signed up for six sessions with a personal trainer and began my getting fit regime. I went into it whole heartedly and never really looked back. I also persuaded Martin that perhaps it was not a good idea that we worked together and he should employ someone to do what I was doing in the office. Someone else would be far motivated than me and probably more of an asset. He agreed and my office duties came to a welcome end. In the November I had caught a really nasty chest infection and it lingered until Christmas. I still continued at the gym when I was able to breathe properly. Some weeks were better than others and on the bad weeks I could just about stand up let alone work out, but I was on a mission and I am very determined and would not let a minor setback like a serious illness stand in my way. Before the holidays I had had enough of being ill and going backwards and forwards to the GP who just kept prescribing more and more antibiotics and different strength inhalers. So I called a private doctor who put me on a course of steroids, which I knew would work because they always had for Jodi in the past. Within a few days I felt completely back to normal, except with an extremely large appetite and heaps of energy as that is what the side effects of steroids are.

By the New Year I was back in the gym ready and raring to carry on my undertaking to reach the goals that I had set for myself. My hair was short, my body and mind were changing, and I felt that this year 2003 was a year of dramatic changes. I just hoped that they would be for the good and not the other way. The way things were between Martin and me it could go either way.

Jodi was settled in school and although her development left much cause for concern there was little else that I could do in that period of time that I was not already doing. The other girls were developing strengths and talents of their own and I spent all my after school hours helping them to develop into the best they could be, even if it only meant taking them from one place to another.

Emma's dance teacher had told me that she was a gifted dancer, her piano teacher told me that she was a gifted pianist, everything that she did she was able to do better than expected, and as a result she was probably the most confidant and precocious of all my children. It took as much effort to keep her grounded sometimes as it did to keep Jodi at the level she needed to be at.

These things though, although a challenge, were not really. It was just life. Life does not present everything to you on a plate. If you want the best of it then it is up to you to make it happen. Nothing comes to those that don't help themselves. So Emma was talented because she had the opportunities to show and develop that talent, and it is not just about cost and money, because the classes that I sent her to were not expensive and catered for all children not privileged ones. It is about making time and putting in the effort to make things happen. I was passionate about giving each of my children individual time to develop in areas that were important to them. I guided and helped them and never made it a problem to take them where they needed to be. I never made them feel that it was too much trouble and they in turn had the confidence to pursue their dreams too.

Tamara also danced, but was still very little and was happy to be with me and let me read to her and tell her stories and help her with her homework. That was enough for her. Sasha swam and ran with an athletic club three or four times a week, and Jodi along with all her therapies had singing lessons to help with her breathing and speech and it also turned out that she had perfect pitch.

So life should have been wonderful and to a certain extent it was. The only thing that now needed serious consideration was my marriage, and that for me was going to need significant thought about how to make that the best that it could be.

CHAPTER 49

Sasha represented Great Britain in a Jewish International Athletics competition in Houston, USA that summer. My parents came with us to support her and my Aunty Gloria and Uncle Harry drove from North Carolina to be with us too. The competition was wonderful and Sasha and the team came away with several gold, silver and bronze medals. We then flew to New Jersey where she competed in a swimming competition and once again she swam beautifully and came away with several medals.

When the competition was over we took the children to Orlando where we met up with our Leeds friends Debbie, David and her family. One night as I sat speaking to Debbie I realised that the trip for Martin and me had not been so wonderful. However wonderful it was to see our daughter compete and do so well, our relationship was not going the same way. I think on reflection that it was actually my fault, because the last fifteen years had changed me. It had been a gradual process initially and I had been so busy raising my children that it didn't really notice. I had probably been very careful not to upset the equilibrium of our family life, so was careful not to address any uncertainties that I may have had, but suddenly I felt that I needed to be who I wanted to be and I wanted my opinions heard and taken into account. This for Martin was a shock to his system and he didn't quite know how to respond. He was very defensive and very argumentative, and although I often gave in to him to avoid complete meltdown, I always made sure that he heard what I had to say first. So our quiet little happy home was no longer that, and my children were beginning to notice or maybe they had noticed for a while, but now they were beginning to voice their concerns.

The holiday for Martin and me was not a success, and when we returned home I suggested it was time that perhaps we needed some help and so we enlisted the help of a counsellor. Opening up to a stranger for anyone is extremely difficult. I personally felt inhibited and a little embarrassed, but I tried my best to speak from my heart and express my true and real concerns about how my life had been until then. But I had been through this before so much of it was not new to me. The real purpose for us going was so that Martin would be able to lay some of his ghosts to rest, and deal with issues from his past so that he could move on and become a better person as a result. He found it almost impossible to open up. It was as if he were going through the motions just to make me happy. He spoke about the boys and how the loss of having sons had impacted his life, and that his relationships with other people, especially Nicholas and Stephanie, were affected as a result of the fact that they had sons. He spoke of how he found it difficult to accept that he had a child that had learning difficulties and the fact that she would never have a normal life was something that he found almost impossible to come to terms with. Throughout all our sessions though I felt as though he was telling a story and that the person that he was speaking about was not actually in the room. I spoke about my feelings of loss and the support that I felt he had denied me, not necessarily with the loss of the boys because I do feel that grief is so personal and I actually felt as though support or interference from him would have almost been like an intrusion; he could not possibly have known my pain just like I could not know his. I wanted what I felt for my baby boys to be mine and no one else's and so I could not let him share that grief or pain, not even the love that I still held dear to my heart for them. I knew that for me that flame would and could never die and I didn't either expect or want him to understand that. What I needed support for was the fact that we had this child that although was full of potential, needed specialist help to reach it, and I needed him to help me to help her to achieve it, but because he was so in denial everything that I suggested was such a battle and I found it all so frustrating. It is probably one of my biggest faults, but when I believe that something is the right or correct path I find it very difficult to back down. Especially when it concerns my children. In the past I gave in for a quiet easy life, even though in my head I knew it was not what I would have done, and although on the outside it seemed that I had backed down, in my head I knew that I hadn't really because the path that was chosen was not the one I would have selected.

Now, however, I seemed to have found my voice. I was more focused and more assertive than I had ever been. Rightly or wrongly I wanted things my way for a change. So the sessions with the counsellor became quite heated and on occasions quite comical, but what was emerging was that there had been so much that had happened and we had dealt with our lives so completely separately that I had grown from him. He no longer represented a husband and a rock, a safe place and secure haven. I thought of him as a child and brother, someone that needed my full attention and support. I had grown away from him; the grief, the pain, the tests that our lives had thrown in our path were taking their toll. I had grown into a different person, my dreams had changed or maybe they just had not been realised. Maybe he was unable to be the person that I needed or maybe I just didn't need anyone, but one thing I felt at the time for absolute certainty was that I did not want to be with him for the rest of my life. I felt that he would only be another needy person in my life to take care of, and he would never be able to provide me with what I needed. I don't think I ever really knew what that was, and perhaps I still don't, but I did know what it was that I didn't need.

That night on the last day of November 2003 we told the children that we were splitting up, that we had grown apart and that although we still cared very much for each other, we were more like brother and sister not husband and wife. I have never felt so guilty in my life. I felt I was causing more pain than they could ever know how to cope with and my heart broke for them, but I kept saying to myself that other children had survived broken homes and so would mine. I would make it right for them, that somehow the pain would pass and they would carry on their lives to be well adjusted wonderful adults and they would not spend the rest of their lives hating and resenting me for taking away their security.

Martin gathered his belongings and moved out that night; this tragedy was my doing, I had inflicted this pain onto my children and the guilt was almost too much to bear. I couldn't get over it, there was nothing that would make me feel right about this decision, and yet I couldn't see another way.

CHAPTER 50

The next three months were the most surreal I had ever experienced. Initially Martin was very angry with me for taking away his family and he felt that my motives were not genuine. He told people that I must have been having an affair and that nothing else could be reason enough for me to have behaved the way that I had.

My children cried a great deal, and I made a huge amount of soup. I wanted the house to smell homely when they came home from school so that they would not have that empty out of sorts feeling that I was feeling in the pit of my stomach all the time. The guilt never subsided it just grew and grew. I even felt guilty that I was hurting Martin so much and I felt that I had brought this on my family.

Sometimes I thought that it would be so much easier to just get back together and put up and shut up, and other times I thought that I had come this far what would be the point of going backwards. I was more than a little confused. Eventually Martin stopped being so volatile and changed his tack. He started being extra nice, but at the same time he started dating lots of different women. I never understood how in one breath he was telling me how much he loved and missed me and in the next he was having sex with another woman. How is that possible? How can men just switch off from their emotions that way? He moved into a beautiful flat in West Hampstead, and my children were quite happy to go and stay there.

One evening he suggested that we go out to dinner to discuss finances and I was to collect him from his place as the children were there for the night. When I walked in and my little girls were all in their pyjamas, playing on the computer and watching television, I felt I was in the movie *Sliding Doors*. It was like I was looking at a parallel life, one that I was not part of and one that functioned without my input, and it made me very uncomfortable and a little jealous. These were my girls, and it felt as though they had been taken away from me. My mind was racing when we sat in the Chinese restaurant round the corner from his flat. I didn't want this life; it was not part of the game plan.

Lying in bed that night once again sleep eluded me, and all I could think of was that if I went through with this divorce then I would not be a total part of my children's life, Martin would not be part of my life at all, only in a financial capacity, and the thing that I found more disturbing than anything else was that if Martin remarried and then died, my children would have to "sit shiva" (a Jewish mourning custom where the immediate family sit on low chairs for a week and people come to pay their respects and pray with them) with his new wife, and I would not be part of them. I was extremely uncomfortable with this thought, however bizarre that may be.

I started work in early February as a welfare assistant for a little boy that had learning difficulties in a nursery in Edgware. I cried the whole way there on the morning that I started. Martin was dating in full swing and I hated it. I don't know if it would have been quite so bad if I was doing the same, but I had not even ventured out of my front door of an evening. I would light candles and drink little half bottles of wine and tell myself that I was finding myself, and that this was a necessary part of the healing process. I am surprised that my eyes were even visible because I had cried so much over the last few months, and I don't remember one time when I thought that things were getting easier. My only comfort was my children and every other weekend they would go off to his flat and not return until the Sunday, unless of course Martin had a hot date and then they would be returned on the Saturday night, because I was always home, and if on the odd occasion I had plans to go out with my married friends, then Jodi was happy to babysit. I suppose Martin wanted his flat vacated in case he needed to bring one of his dates back there. It certainly would not be very cool to have his four daughters as the welcoming committee!

I had seen a house around the corner that I had made an offer on and I had someone that was interested in buying the house that we were living in. My mum had come to stay to help me sort through the rubbish and pack up what needed to be taken. I felt that I was in a complete daze. I was so desperately unhappy; this was a thousand times worse than being in an unhappy marriage. Everything felt unnatural. I kept saying to myself that a year down the line I would feel much better, but I on the other hand wasn't sure if I would make it to a year down the line. This was like nothing that I had ever experienced. When I lost the babies it was not directly my doing, and once they had been born there was nothing that I could do that would change the outcome of what happened next. With Jodi the most that I could do was to source the correct programmes and opportunities to make her life the best that it could be, even the court case was something that I had to deal with because the situation was forced upon me, but this situation now was directly in my control. I could change its course and return to the comfort of the familiar instead of this whirlwind of change that was so alien to me.

Every time I thought of Martin with another woman my insides seemed to constrict and I felt sick with jealousy and wanted them to know that they could never be as good as I was in bed. I am sure that is not quite true, but in those nights alone when I relived the best of our sex I knew that I was quite good at it. Because when you have been with someone for as long as we had been together sex was uninhibited, there was nothing that was embarrassing or taboo. We knew each other and our bodies inside out and that knowledge takes years to acquire. I also knew categorically that I would never let another man see my body; it was ugly and scarred and I could never feel confident enough in another relationship to take off my clothes. So with all of that in mind I suppose many of my emotions were also a result of the fact that I had been celibate for over three months, probably nearer to six, and I was very, very horny, so I wonder now when looking back if this fact may have also clouded my vision a little.

My mum took me to see our rabbi because I had finally reached the stage where I just did not know what to do next. I was about to exchange on the house and I really hated the thought of moving, I was in a job that I really didn't want to be in, my children were not as happy and settled as they should have been, and I had changed their perspective on life forever. My husband turned up in something new and trendy every time he came to my door; I couldn't understand why he was unable to dress himself like that when we were together. I was uncomfortable with the feelings that were stirred every time I thought of him with another woman, and I was even more disturbed by the fact that I kept imagining having sex with him again and getting quite aroused by the thought. Although I decided that I probably would leave that part out when speaking to the rabbi!

The rabbi was quite direct when he told me that once I was divorced I would have absolutely no right to ask Martin for anything other than what is stipulated in the divorce papers. I could not expect him to pick up or take the children anywhere if it is not his day to see them, and I should expect that he will be remarried in a very short space of time. None of this sat well with me and I went home feeling even more bemused. I spent the night crying once again, and although I knew that he was seeing his girlfriend I sent him a text saying that I thought it was very sad that our lives had turned out this way and that I wished it could be different.

The next day he called me in my break and arranged to meet me at home for lunch. On the way home I popped in to see Stephanie and quickly relayed the rabbi's words to her and her friend that happened to be there having lunch. Her friend said that everyone deserved a second chance and that when I met Martin I should tell him that I wanted him back immediately. I don't know why but those were the words that seemed to make more sense than anyone else's, and I knew that the advice that she gave that day was the right thing to do.

I walked into the house and Martin was waiting with fresh bread and a cup of tea. As soon as he opened the door to me I said that it was enough and I wanted him back warts and all and then I kissed him. It was the first kiss I had had in such a long time and it felt like I had come home.

When I told the girls that their father was moving home it was as if someone had come and drawn back the curtains from their eyes. I had not seen their eyes so bright for so many months, and they were truly happy and I knew that for them this was the best thing that could happen.

When our paths had split the day that Benjamin had died I was not sure if they would ever meet again. Fifteen years later they merged once again and when we made love that night I felt that we connected in a way that had not happened since probably before we were trying to have a baby.

Perhaps we were actually sole mates, perhaps our lives were so intertwined that whatever went on, and whoever we became, we could not actually live without each other, or I could not live without him. I was fully aware that he was living very well without me. I decided to ignore that fact as it would in no way benefit our new found passion.

So he moved back home and life soon resumed and normality set in and all was calm once again. I felt that I could breathe and sleep and do all those things that I was unable to think about in the last few months. My house became the usual hubbub of activity and my children had a spring in their steps once again. When we sat around the table on a Friday night, the Sabbath candles burning in the background, the excited chatter of my girls relaying events of the week, eyes shining and skins glowing with secure satisfaction, I thought to myself that it was not for me to deprive them of this. This was their right, we had brought them into this world and they deserved the best. They deserved to sleep at night knowing that we were doing our best to give them the best. I knew categorically then that my life could never be as important as theirs, and although I undoubtedly wanted happiness and fulfilment for myself, it could never be and would never be at their expense.

CHAPTER 51

Time moved swiftly on and for a while things were idyllic. We bought a beautiful holiday flat in Israel, Martin's business was booming, and our relationship had never been better. I enjoyed spending time with Martin and we would meet regularly for lunch or would go out for dinner alone, but we made a real effort to hold onto that honeymoon feeling that we had rekindled when we had first moved back together. I used to say to people that for us splitting up was the best thing that we had ever done because we were able to correct our mistakes and give each other a chance to revalue the relationship, and then try to change the things that had not been right. One thing though that I did learn was that a leopard cannot change its spots, and whilst you can change a situation and also change things that you do, it is not possible to really change who you are. Although for me I had found a part of myself that I didn't know existed and that person till this day is still growing, I am still the same person deep down, with the same insecurities and the same strengths and weaknesses; it's just that now I am learning how to make the best of myself and use both my good and bad assets to try and make me a better person and to use my experiences to help me through the rest of my life.

By the end of 2003 we knew that we would have to start thinking about Jodi's future. She was definitely not going to be able to access higher education without support and whatever she did choose it would certainly not be academic. The other thing that we had to take into consideration was that she was a vulnerable girl. She had the body of a woman and the mind of a child, she was easily persuaded, and didn't really understand the long-term implications of her actions. I couldn't send her to a mainstream college, she would not last a minute, and she was not severe enough for a local special needs college. There seemed to be no middle ground.

It was like Dr Millett had said, the Jewish community will make sure that there is a place for her to go, because one day when visiting Michelle and Neville they introduced us to some friends of theirs that had a boy thirteen years before we had had Jodi and he had difficulties that were on a very similar level to Jodi's. They also had despaired about his future and so they had searched out other families who had children in the same position and had started a Jewish residential college for young people with mild to moderate learning difficulties in Manchester. It was aimed at giving these young people a chance of independence, and the aim was to ensure that whatever the potential of the young person, the college would ensure that it was achieved. I expressed my concerns that I felt that Jodi would not cope with being away from the family and his reply was that there came a time in the life of a child that had learning difficulties when the parents had to stop thinking about themselves and start thinking only and totally about the good of their child. I heard what he said, took it on board, but I did have reservations about it being the best thing for Jodi. Undoubtedly anything would be better than her sitting at home every day with no friends or social life, but I was unsure about her coping without me. It is not that I was disillusioned about our relationship and that I thought that I had been so fantastic, it was just that I knew Jodi well enough to know that even going to stay with my mum and being away for a night or two was difficult for her. I did, however, discuss it with her and she was keen to go and have a look to see what they had to offer.

I made all the necessary enquiries about funding and thought that it would no doubt be a battle to convince the authorities that this was the right place for her if indeed we did choose to send her there. There actually was no alternative.

We went to look at the college at the end of 2004 and left Jodi there overnight to have an assessment. Martin and I stayed in a hotel not far from the college and actually for us it was a really lovely break. I did not like to leave the children so soon after our split if I didn't have to. I felt that their lives had been disrupted enough in the last few years and I just wanted everyone to be settled and secure and for us to go away would not be conducive to this. So for Martin and me it was an extremely welcome break.

When we collected Jodi the following afternoon she was so excited about the prospect of going to this college. She said that she had met lots of lovely people and when I asked what she thought their needs were she said that she couldn't tell that there was anything wrong with any of them. That for me was a sign that it was the right place for her. She felt that she fitted in here which is something that she had never felt before. It was for me the moment that I realised that I had probably done all that I could for her and that realisation was quite a poignant thought. I felt almost redundant, and a little empty. I felt as though someone was about to take over my life's work, and I was possessive over it and I did not like the emotions that were stirring inside me. We had lunch in the college with all the students and Jodi sat engaged and smiling amongst them. I felt the lump in my throat and my eyes well as I saw her for what she really was, a little lost soul searching for her niche and suddenly she was sat with people that she could relate to and that could relate to her. They all spoke the same language and even though the content of their conversation was not what you would expect to hear from young people of this age who were sitting around a table, for them anything else would have been unnatural.

Jodi kept in touch with all her new found friends and they came to visit during the school holidays. She even went out for lunch with one of the boys from the college. Her little face shone with hope and excitement as she tried to imagine a completely different world opening up for her. For me I had mixed emotions. How could I let this child woman leave the safety net of her home and move into a world that I was unable to really be part of? How would either of us cope, because whilst she was around she enabled me to have a function. Whilst the others were at school I spent my days taking her from one place to another, listening to her daily dramas, helping her to achieve the things that she found so difficult, and whilst I was doing all those things I had a very important purpose. Without her there my life would be ordinary, my other girls were growing and fast becoming independent little souls. They needed me for guidance and support, and of course to be a taxi service, and that is exactly how it should be, but I wasn't used to normal, there had been nothing normal in my life so far, and I wasn't sure how I would cope with that.

I started running and signed up to do the London Marathon. That would be sure to change my focus. It really was a wonderful release and an even better personal challenge. The thought terrified me, but I knew that I had the strength of character to complete this mad challenge. It certainly took my mind away from the empty nest syndrome that was fast approaching.

I had never been so physically fit; I was training three times a week with a trainer and running three days when I was not training, with one day off. Everyone told me that I was obsessed, but I really didn't care, I loved the results. I had achieved what I had set out to do that summer in Spain and now I set myself new challenges every day. It kept me focused, energetic and slim, how could that be a bad thing! I felt that all of a sudden somewhere in the midst of dramas and chaos I had discovered that I actually mattered. Not only that, I liked the feeling that I mattered. Guilty stirrings rose up sometimes when I thought that perhaps I was spending too much time thinking about myself, and my own personal achievements, but I soon suppressed those thoughts when I had that wonderful high after a really good run or a particularly good training session. My body had never looked so good, in clothes that is. The scars of my pregnancies would never heal both outwardly and inwardly, but I was beginning to feel as though I should like myself and acknowledge the things that I had achieved, and perhaps by doing this I would gain in confidence and self-belief.

Looking back over the years and as a result of my experiences I am sure that I was probably acquiring the ability to like myself and also trust my own judgement without actually consciously making that effort, but it was only during this latest period of my life that I realised it on a conscious level. I suddenly felt almost empowered and I felt that I had gained an inner strength and insight that I would have never known had my life taken me down a different path.

During my fitness regime I was also in constant communication with the local authority. Jodi was going from the LEA to Connexions and child services, so all the funding reports and statements had to be handed over and she had to be reassessed. We were extremely lucky because the person that was in charge of our case was extremely sympathetic, and fought our corner the whole way. We actually received the funding we needed to send Jodi to Langdon College (the college in Manchester) and it was a relatively stress free accomplishment. The decision was now made: she would leave the home that I had worked so hard to create and she would enter a world that was completely new and alien to her. A world without cuddles and reassurances, the kind of things only a mother can give her child. Nothing can replace this bond or feeling, and it is only through life experiences that we are able as people to move on from the needs that only a mother can provide. But Jodi had had none of the life experiences that would help her on her way to this new independence and I was unable to prepare her for them as I didn't know what it was that she needed to achieve this mental state.

Whilst I was filled with excitement for this new phase, hoping with all my soul that this would be the place that would give Jodi the happiness and the tools to cope with the rest of her life in a way that I could not do for her, I knew that this was going to be as hard for me as it was going to be for her. My runs increased and my training became more intense; they were at the time my life-line, they were my crutch and my scaffolding, and without these things I think I may have crumbled. I marvelled at the way life almost hands you lifelines when you most need them. The trick is to recognise them and then grab them.

In the April I ran the London Marathon. I thought that I had never been so nervous about anything else. I could not imagine that I would ever complete it. All the training and preparing seemed to have paled into insignificance; you can't train yourself not to be nervous and I was terrified. I woke in the morning at five and did not stop crying until I was collected by the taxi that was also picking up Neville and four other male runners. They said that they were all as nervous as I was, but they had done it before so knew what to expect. They knew that they would finish the course; they also knew how hard it was going to be. I regretted the decision to run the whole journey to the start. I kept asking myself what would possess a person to put themselves through this and what an earth was I thinking when I signed up for this challenge. My stomach was in knots, I couldn't imagine that this day would ever be over and I wanted to kick myself for getting into this situation.

As soon as I started running, my nerves dispersed and I concentrated solely on the task ahead. It was as though I had convinced my brain that this was going to happen and that there would be an end to it and I was going to achieve what I had set out to do. I had once again overcome the challenge of my dreadful nervousness and I started the run with quiet determination. The atmosphere was like nothing that I had ever experienced. It was just incredible the number of people that turned out on the streets to support the runners. It was an honour to be running in such an amazing event. I remember thinking that with all this good in so many people and all this camaraderie it was incredible that there was so much bad in this world. It was the most physically enduring thing that I had ever done, but thanks to my wonderful trainer Dean, and of course my body for not giving up on me, I completed the London Marathon in five hours and three minutes. As I crossed the bridge to have my time chip cut from my shoe I cried from relief and disbelief and I was completely overcome with emotion, but the first thought that came into my head was I can't wait to do this again next year!

My supporters were waiting for me in the meeting area; they were all my wonderful family and we went home for steak and champagne. For me that day instilled me with confidence and became a turning point in my self-esteem. Although I had a fantastic support system in place, I had only myself to rely on and there was no one that could help me reach the finish line on the day except myself. I had overcome my nerves and faced a personal challenge and I was actually really proud of myself. I wore my medal with pride and only took it off when I went to bed that night!

CHAPTER 52

Jodi was set to start Langdon College in September 2005. Just after the London Marathon she started complaining of back pain. I dismissed it for a while because as with all children they are usually complaining about something or another. However, this pain seemed to be becoming worse so I took her to see the back surgeon who had been monitoring her scoliosis over the past thirteen years and who had recently signed her off. He took x-rays and scans to find out if anything really was wrong. I didn't think that there was a possibility that there was anything serious and suspected that she may need a course of physiotherapy, but I was wrong this time and it turned out that she had a fracture in one of the vertebrae in her lower back and she would need surgery using metal pins and rods to repair it.

I know I was wrong to feel sorry for my situation, but it just seemed that every time things were calm and settled and life was taking on a relatively normal course something would pop up to once again test us. Spinal surgery is major; it is not a week off and then all back to normal. It is at least a six to eight week rehab programme and that is after the initial recovery period.

So Jodi didn't start Langdon in September, instead she had surgery. She just about passed as a paediatric so we had her surgery at the Portland. It was the first time she had been admitted for eleven years and the first time that I had been back there since I had had Tamara. We took the lift up to the sixth floor and as the doors opened a wave of nostalgia hit me, the smells, the memories, everything was in front of me as though it were yesterday that I was riding the lift to see my babies that fought so hard to live. It is so hard to describe the tears that welled up for they are not the same as those one sheds when watching a sad movie. These came from so deep inside, they came from a place that I thought was buried and they rose to the surface so quickly that they were uncontrollable. I felt my chest knot around my heart as though the muscles were protecting it from breaking more, the emotion was so immense that I almost had to gasp for breath. It took me a while to compose myself, but once I had I was fine and once again focused on the task at hand.

It was another harrowing and upsetting week. The surgery went to plan, and Jodi recovered well, but she needed intravenous medication. Unfortunately, because of all the blood gases and tests that she had endured in the first six months of her life her veins were terrible and they had to keep moving the site of the drips, and each time they did it took them several attempts. Jodi found the whole ordeal quite distressing. While she was on the morphine drip her oxygen levels kept dropping and I would lie in bed listening to the sound of her breathing and the alarms going off every so often as her levels became dangerously low, reliving the experience of seventeen years earlier. She was supposed to be in hospital for a week to ten days, but after four days she had had enough and decided that she would rather recover at home. So she persuaded the nurses to let her walk up the stairs because they would only let her home if she could safely go up and down stairs. We went home that afternoon.

Eight weeks later, after rigid rehab programmes, we took Jodi to Manchester to start at Langdon. Once again my insides were in knots. I felt that this child that I had rarely been separated from was being taken from me. I knew in my head that was not the case, but my heart wouldn't listen and it felt like it was being pulled in two. Part of me was excited for her to embark on this new chapter of her life and the other felt like it had all happened too quickly. I was not ready to be entering this time of my life. Where had the days of nappies and teething gone? It seemed as though everything had gone by so fast I had not noticed. One minute I was willing life into this child and the next she was leaving home to start on a period of her life that did not involve me as her primary carer. Although I would have constant contact, the decision of what she had to eat or where she went and how she got there would no longer be mine. These functions that had become part of my life were about to change and this made me feel empty but excited, liberated but alone, all at the same time. I couldn't bear the thought of her not coming down to the breakfast table every morning or kissing her goodnight each evening. With Jodi it was not a natural progression. Most teenagers by the time they reached the age of seventeen are out and about, and home is usually the place they see the least of, so whilst it would be a wrench when any child leaves home, they have already had periods of absence. But with Jodi it was different, she was always home, she was a permanent fixture and now all of a sudden she was leaving and the thought of the space that she would leave was almost too much to bear.

We drove to Manchester and I familiarised her and myself with the area and her room, we put up the pictures of the family on her wall and I unpacked her clothes. I delayed the moment of goodbye as long as I could, but eventually like all time it had to come. This was the moment that I had probably dreaded from the minute she was born. When she had started nursery and they pulled her from my arms kicking and screaming I couldn't imagine that the feeling could ever be any worse, until now. As she stood on the doorstep of her new home sobbing and waving, holding the hand of one of the wonderful staff, I tried my best to smile back encouragingly telling her that it would only be a short time till we were together again. I sat in the car sobbing silently all the way home. There were and are still no words to describe that emptiness that I felt, that feeling that somehow I had failed her. I couldn't do what the College was promising, and because of that I had to send my daughter away into the care of strangers. They knew better than I did how to help my child take the next steps and I felt frustrated yet grateful.

The next few weeks my runs became longer and my exercise became more regimented. Some days I felt liberated, and others I couldn't stop crying. It took me a while to stop thinking that cooking meals was pointless as not all the family were together, but as with everything normality and routine set in. Jodi called me at least twenty times a day. I think I actually had more conversations with her whilst she was away than I did when she was here. She was happy and so I felt content that I had done the right thing.

Langdon was the best thing that had happened to her in a long time and she had friends and a real life. She was active every day and she was functioning at a level that suited her. She blossomed and grew as a result and we could see a light at the end of our tunnel.

Jodi had to go back under the knife in the February after she had started the college as she was allergic to the metal rods that they had used to repair the original fracture. So that was another recovery and weeks at home. It seemed that she would never settle into the life at college, and it seemed that I would never have the normal life that I was so afraid of.

Sasha took her GCSEs that summer and worked tirelessly in order to achieve the grades that would ensure her future. She then went on tour for a month to Israel with an organisation. Once again I felt that finality. That change of tides as one era ended and another began. This child of mine who had been grown up for so many years was actually growing into her years now and was an independent determined being who knew exactly what direction she was heading and how she was getting there. My role was no longer that of carer for her, I could now only advise and discuss, the decisions that she made from this point would have to be hers and hers alone. Her mistakes, her accomplishments would be down to her and as a parent my role was now to sit back and be there to support her every move.

The blissful harmony that had been restored the day that Martin returned seemed to be under threat once again, and although I chose to ignore the signs they were slowly beginning to show themselves in subtle ways. He found the fact that he could not dictate the choices that our children made very difficult. He did not approve of some of Sasha's choices and found it hard to let her make her own mistakes. As I said in the past, a leopard never changes his spots, and control was one of Martin's spots. Martin became totally engrossed in planning Emma's bat mitzvah, which was wonderful for me as I didn't have very much to do with the arrangements except to approve the ideas and occasionally email the planner. Martin made several trips backwards and forwards to Israel and loved the control that I was giving him. He was completely obsessed with the planning of this event and I was happy for him to be that way.

In August 2006 we made Emma's bat mitzvah in Israel. Once again it was completely different from the other two that we had made. Emma loved the attention and the opportunity to perform. She was and still is a natural performer, singing, dancing and entertaining 90 per cent of the time. We danced on the beach and walked through ruins and mountains. We provided coaches, drink and food for our guests and had a week of wonderful festivities. Martin and I were really happy, enjoying each other and our surroundings and ignoring the stresses and strains that were beginning to creep back into our lives. It was a truly wonderful week and when it was over I had a week of relaxing on the beach, soaking in the warmth of the sun and sea, thinking and planning for the year ahead, and making resolutions that would help me through my days. I looked forward to the possibility of normal and boredom, but somehow knew that would not be my destiny.

On our return to England Jodi started to complain about back pain again. This time the cause could not be located. Three weeks after she had returned to college she was sent home. She was admitted into hospital and no reason for the pain was found. The pain spread to all over her body and she was unable to tolerate temperature change. She was constantly freezing and her hands and feet were like ice. We took her to a different specialist and she spent a considerable amount of time in hospital and I spent a considerable amount of time travelling backwards and forwards. She was unable to go to college and for a while she was in a wheelchair. The doctors were at a loss as to what may have caused all these reactions so they gave her copious amounts of medication. She was on anti-convulsion pills, pills that stopped inflammation, antidepressants and ordinary paracetamol.

To add to all of this Emma was diagnosed with glandular fever and Martin had a hernia. Looking back now the whole thing seemed somewhat comical and at the time I think I laughed about it because otherwise I think I may have developed some suicidal behaviour patterns. Actually, that would never have been an option, but I did marvel at the way so much can happen and go wrong to one family.

One day Sasha said to me that I must be a very good person, because according to Jewish law only the great rabbis and the very good people of the world were tested whilst living on this earth. Everyone else had their tests after they had died before they were admitted into the pearly gates. I decided that I would rather not be such a good person especially as I was not convinced about the after-life. I thought the amount of tests that were being bestowed upon us was ridiculous and it was about time someone gave us a break. I decided that my thoughts would have to become a little less pure, perhaps that would help!

Jodi was never diagnosed, and because every single test was coming out with a negative result I decided on the advice of my physiotherapist to get her off the drugs and moving as quickly as possible. So I became stricter and made her start exercising and we gave away the wheelchair. I would not listen to moans and groans and with the help of Dean my personal trainer we gave Jodi a programme of simple exercises that would start her moving normally again. Suggestion with Jodi had always been my most powerful tool. If I told her that it would be better for her to jump from a bridge then to watch television her love and trust was so great that she would do it. So she listened to what I had to say about her recovery and took it on board. Three months later she completed an eleven mile walk to raise money for Langdon College and community. Martin and I walked alongside her and her determination and sense of achievement was immense. It was this attitude and fight that has seen Jodi through so many challenges and through her I think we have all learnt something that we could never have had she not been there to teach us. She has touched the hearts and lives of so many and the world is a better place because of her.

Martin had his hernia operated on and he recovered reasonably quickly although we did have to have daily inspections to see what colour the bruising had become. I had never spent so much time inspecting those regions and decided that I really didn't enjoy that activity. Martin and I seemed to be struggling again. Actually, I think it was me that was struggling. As long as I gave him enough attention and sex and fulfilled his needs, which I more often than not did, Martin was oblivious to my well being. That is not to say he did not adore me, he did, and he would do anything to make me happy, it's just that sometimes his complexities and obsessions and mountain of issues stood between us and I had to be in a certain frame of mind to deal with all of it. Eventually it all came to a head as it did before and we were once again working to save our marriage and our family unit, but this time the power of communication played a very important role and I no longer swept things under the carpet for a quiet life. I was direct with Martin and he did seem to take on board what I was saying and started trying harder to control his behaviour to suit the needs of the family. As mentioned on numerous occasions, people don't change, things do, and that is all I will ever be able to ask of Martin. Even that is a very tall order.

Emma slowly improved and within a few months she was able to resume with her normal activities. She had all sorts of tests and although she still suffers from regular headaches and migraine it was thought that she will one day grow out of all the symptoms.

Eventually things became a version of normal. All the children were following the paths that they should, our home became calm once again, there were no major health issues or educational issues, and I was able to sit back and assess my journey, and also where I thought I should go from here. Finally I was at the point in my life when I could do something for myself and yet I felt that I needed to put to use the roads that I had travelled. I felt that out of the rollercoaster of events that I had experienced something good had to come of it. There had to be a way of using them all to help and give comfort to others whilst at the same time fulfilling my need to become an independent and assertive woman. I had become a person that had the capabilities to achieve goals and climb mountains, and I needed to let the world know that whilst there is an abundance of bad, out of it somewhere along the line will come good. It may be only that you have dealt with it, and it still lingers, or it may be that you have managed to be rid of the bad and replaced it with something good. Sometimes I think people should know that things happen and often it is not the way you would have liked but always it has to be dealt with. I felt that although I was the same person, somewhere deep inside I had grown over the years. I had become more focused and learnt to hide my vulnerability, and most importantly I actually believed in myself. I have become someone I never thought that I could be. I am stronger more determined and focused then the person that entered into holy matrimony all those years ago. I feel as though I have held onto this family against all odds and fought to give each one of my girls the best of me and all that I can give. I have come to terms with grief and loss, and faced challenges that I never thought that I would be able to endure. I have taken all of these things and I am determined to make a life from it by using this book and my experiences, and conveying them to other people so that perhaps they may take some of it and use it to make something good happen in their lives.

Life today is by no means normal. My marriage is a challenge and I think will always remain so, whilst my children are to me the most beautiful in the world both inside and out and a credit to us as parents. They bring pleasure and joy to my life every minute of every day.

Jodi will be entering the Langdon Community in July 2008 where she will receive whatever support she needs to live an independent life. She will be around the corner in Edgware so she will be able to spend as much time with the family as she wants. She has had numerous boyfriends and is quite the social animal, and as long as she has the space to listen to her music, watch her movies and read her books at least five times over, she is as happy as a sand boy.

Sasha is about to fly the nest. She is taking a gap year next year and then off to university. Life without Sasha at home is going to be quite an adjustment, but I feel that I have the strength of character to make that change.

Emma is a talented, bright child who brings light and sunshine into everyone's life. She is smart and funny and knows exactly what she wants and where she is heading.

Tamara is my sensitive, sweet yet determined flower. She is my youngest child and therefore my baby and for the foreseeable future I can't imagine that changing.

Martin is learning to deal with his issues. I think he has a mountain to climb, but he is aware of that and determined to climb it.

Who knows what the future holds for me, but I do know that whatever it throws in my path I will cope with its consequences and will not let any challenge beat me.

My journey has made me who I am today and I am proud of that person.

Printed in the United Kingdom
by Lightning Source UK Ltd.
136209UK00001B/254/P